Embracing NEARNESS

Embracing NEARNESS

Unlocking the Power of Divine Conversation

Sephora Pierre-Louis

EMBRACING NEARNESS
Copyright © 2025 by Sephora Pierre-Louis

All rights reserved. Neither this publication nor any part of this publication may be reproduced or transmitted in any form or by any means, electronic or mechanical, including photocopying, recording or any information storage and retrieval system, without permission in writing from the author.

Unless otherwise indicated, all scripture quotations are taken from the Holy Bible, New International Version®, NIV®. Copyright © 1973, 1978, 1984, 2011 by Biblica, Inc.™ Used by permission of Zondervan. All rights reserved worldwide. www.zondervan.com The "NIV" and "New International Version" are trademarks registered in the United States Patent and Trademark Office by Biblica, Inc.™ Scripture quotations marked (NKJV) taken from the New King James Version®. Copyright © 1982 by Thomas Nelson. Used by permission. All rights reserved. Scripture quotations marked (NLT) are taken from the Holy Bible, New Living Translation, copyright ©1996, 2004, 2015 by Tyndale House Foundation. Used by permission of Tyndale House Publishers, Carol Stream, Illinois 60188. All rights reserved. Scripture quotations are from the ESV® Bible (The Holy Bible, English Standard Version®), © 2001 by Crossway, a publishing ministry of Good News Publishers. Used by permission. All rights reserved. The ESV text may not be quoted in any publication made available to the public by a Creative Commons license. The ESV may not be translated in whole or in part into any other language. Scripture quotations marked (CEV) are from the Contemporary English Version Copyright © 1991, 1992, 1995 by American Bible Society. Used by Permission. Scripture quotations marked MSG are taken from The Message, copyright © 1993, 2002, 2018 by Eugene H. Peterson. Used by permission of NavPress. All rights reserved. Represented by Tyndale House Publishers.

Printed in Canada

Soft cover ISBN: 978-1-4866-2691-5
Hard cover ISBN: 978-1-4866-2693-9
eBook ISBN: 978-1-4866-2692-2

Word Alive Press
119 De Baets Street Winnipeg, MB R2J 3R9
www.wordalivepress.ca

Cataloguing in Publication information can be obtained from Library and Archives Canada.

CONTENTS

DEDICATION	ix
FOREWORD	xi
Introduction A JOURNEY OF FAITH AND PRAYER	xiii
Part One WHAT IS PRAYER?	1
Part Two PERSONAL PRAYERS	39
Part Three PRAYERS FOR OTHERS	125
Part Four THE TWELVE STEPS WITH JESUS	157
Conclusion A LIFE LED BY PRAYER	163
ABOUT THE AUTHOR	167

DEDICATION

To God, who has given me everything, this book is a testament to His boundless grace and mercy. As the Word of God reminds us in James 1:17, *"Every good and every perfect gift is from above, and comes down from the Father of lights, with whom there is no variation or shadow of turning"* (NKJV). Every blessing in my life, including the creation of this book, is a gift from God. Truly, all is grace.

To my great teachers in the school of life—Maxo, my spouse—and my cherished children, Anne, Fayika, and Yolanda, I dedicate this book to you. To my cousin Lumene, who is like a sister to me, thank you for your unconditional love, patience, and unwavering belief in me.

To my church family—the Women's Ministry at Ward Memorial Baptist Church (WMBC)—and especially my dear sisters in the Lord, Sister Lara, Sister Pam, Sister Christine, and Sister Yvonne: Thank you for your invaluable guidance, your wisdom, and the care you've shown in nurturing my spiritual journey. I am deeply grateful to my mentor and pastor, Jusuf Wijaya, for his spiritual leadership. Special thanks to my sister's church, Standard Holiness, and to Pastor Gary, Sister Helen, Sister Bianca, and Sister Dolores for their abundant love and support. To RHEMA college promotion, and Mamiche, my dear supporter, thank you.

To my lifelong friend Guerlyne. Our more than forty years of friendship have been a treasure beyond words. To Warrine Coffey, who has been more than a friend, like a mother to me—thank you for your constant encouragement and love, and to her husband, Bill, for his kindness and support. To David and Taylor, thank you for your trust and love.

To my Plastic Bank family and friends, especially David, Taylor, Shaun, Gidget, Peter, and Karla, thank you for your trust, support, and love towards me.

To my dear friends Nancy, Bryce, Julia, and Anna, your friendship is a cherished gift. To the NAMISEF group—Nahomie, my sister in the Lord, Mirlande, and Florence—and to my journey through the twelve steps with Jesus alongside my dear friend Kareen and my sponsor Naika, thank you for your unwavering companionship. To my doula friend, Christine Frackelton, thank you for walking this path of faith and enlightenment with me.

To my Toastmasters and Partners communities—my mentors, coaches, mentees, and friends—thank you for challenging, inspiring, and helping me grow. I dedicate this first book to you, and to all the readers who will encounter these words. May this book bring you answers, hope, and encouragement.

FOREWORD

It is my privilege to write this foreword for Sephora's debut book, *Embracing Nearness: Unlocking the Power of Divine Conversation*. As her pastor, I've witnessed firsthand Sephora's unwavering passion, commitment, and dedication to prayer. It infuses every page of this remarkable book, which presents a masterful blend of biblical insight, practical application, and accessibility. It is also easy to read and understand!

After reading this manuscript, I wholeheartedly agree with Sephora's assessment that it transcends a simple collection of prayers. It's a deeply personal reflection of her spiritual journey and a powerful testimony to the transformative impact of consistent, heartfelt prayer.

I invite you to join Sephora on this life-changing journey as she generously shares her faith, personal walk, and conversations with God, her perfect heavenly Father. Prepare to be informed, guided, inspired, and transformed.

—Jusuf Wijaya
Pastor

Introduction
A JOURNEY OF FAITH AND PRAYER

I was not born into a Christian family, nor was I taught how to pray as a child. Yet from a very young age I felt the weight of the world pressing down on my shoulders. I was deeply sensitive to everything around me—smells, feelings, impressions, and emotions. I could sense things with an intensity that often left me overwhelmed without fully understanding why. I always had questions, and I needed answers.

When I started going to a primary school run by nuns, prayer was nothing more than a ritual—a series of memorized texts recited without much thought. These prayers left me unfulfilled. I longed for something deeper, something more powerful.

Later I began attending church, but even there I couldn't find the connection I desperately sought, the space where I could pour out my heart, mind, and soul, and emerge feeling renewed.

It wasn't until I surrendered my life to Jesus, accepting Him as my Lord and Savior, that everything began to change. I started to learn how to pray, but at first it still felt hollow, almost silly, to speak to a being I couldn't see or touch. My prayers felt empty.

Have you ever reached a point in your life when your prayers felt empty? When you struggled to find the words, or even stay awake during prayer? Perhaps you're at a stage where your connection with God feels distant, or your prayer life lacks the vitality it once had.

I've known that stage. I understand.

xiii

As I began to read the Word of God, prayer transformed from a one-sided monologue into a two-way conversation with the Almighty. I began to speak to my Lord, and He spoke back to me—through His Word, through nature, and through His people. Prayer became the foundation of my relationship with God, the source of my strength, guidance, and courage to face life's challenges.

> *Prayer became the foundation of my relationship with God, the source of my strength, guidance, and courage to face life's challenges.*

Perhaps it was because my confusion, despair, and lack of answers were so profound that I discovered nothing could harm me while I leaned upon God, asking Him to guide me through every minute of the day. I chose to bring every problem to Him, trusting that He would show me the way forward.

This book is more than a collection of prayers; it is a reflection of my spiritual journey, a testimony to the transformative power of consistent, heartfelt prayer. In these pages, I share the prayers that have not only drawn me closer to God but empowered me to overcome life's obstacles.

This book is also not merely a guide. It is an invitation to deepen your walk with God, trust Him more fully, and experience the profound impact of true conversation with Him.

Before diving into these prayer essentials, I have dedicated some time to explore a series of foundational questions:

- What is prayer?
- Why do I pray?
- Who do I pray to?
- When and how do I pray?

Each section of this book is devoted to a specific area of prayer, whether it's personal petitions or interceding for others. My hope is that these pages will inspire and encourage you, becoming a cherished resource on your spiritual journey.

Part One
WHAT IS PRAYER?

When I was young, I felt that the prayers I was taught were very impersonal, like memorized lessons. In my country, we had to memorize everything—not only our math tables but also history, geography, and grammar. If you had a good memory, you were set for success at test time, even if you didn't understand much or recall anything afterward. You just needed to memorize.

But I always needed more than memorization. Nothing superficial has ever satisfied me. I wanted to go in-depth, to understand, to make sense of things. This is why the memorized prayers at my primary school didn't really resonate with me.

That is, until I discovered that prayer is not a monologue but a dialogue—a conversation between two people. This revelation triggered me to look further to find out who this person was that I was encouraged to have a conversation with.

Still, why would I need to converse with this person? The answer would come later in life when I surrendered my life to my higher power, to my perfect heavenly Father, by accepting the sacrifice of His Son Jesus on the cross to give me eternal life.

God has presented Himself to me as my Creator, the one who knit me in my mother's womb, who created me, who created everything, including the world and everything in it. Psalm 139:13–14 says, *"For you created my inmost being; you knit me together in my mother's womb. I praise you because I am fearfully and wonderfully made; your works are wonderful, I know that full well."* I long to know that God. I long to converse with Him, to get to know Him, to ask questions and get answers. This God has presented Himself to me as someone who has unconditional love for me.

Before that revelation, the concept of unconditional love was vague to me. I had come to the conclusion that love was a concept created to trade, to dominate, to get something out of someone—in the same way that adults loved me as long as I behaved and pleased them. I gave them something (good behaviour) they gave me something in return (affirmation). It was a transaction.

I had to go on a long journey to realize that God, my higher power, does not request anything from me that I am unwilling to give. Why? Because not only does He have it all but He has taken the first step by choosing me and give me everything. John 15:16 reminds us of this freedom: *"You did not choose me, but I chose you and appointed you so that you might go and bear fruit—fruit that will last—and so that whatever you ask in my name the Father will give you."*

Moreover, this God I was learning about gave me the free will to choose to have a relationship with him. I wasn't forced into it. I could decide to go away, to try managing my life as I wished. Or I could ask Him for help.

That was new but exciting.

So I tried to do it all by myself, I became the prodigal girl who tried to manage her life her own way, to the best of her ability—playing perfectionism, wanting to play God, and falling short so many times. I came to the realization that I was powerless over my addictions, over my sins, and my life had become unmanageable.

Wasn't this the first step of the twelve-step program? Where could I find help?

Unshakable help came to me in the person of God the Trinity, revealed as God the Father, God the Son, and God the Holy Spirit. Through John 14:16–17, I was assured of Jesus's promise:

> And I will pray the Father, and He will give you another
> Helper, that He may abide with you forever—the Spirit

of truth, whom the world cannot receive, because it neither sees Him nor knows Him; but you know Him, for He dwells with you and will be in you. (NKJV)

This truth has led me to believe that a power greater than myself can restore me to sanity. I have made the decision to turn my will and life over to the care of God the Trinity, as revealed through the sacrifice of Jesus Christ on the cross, who died so that *"whoever believes in him shall not perish but have eternal life"* (John 3:16).

How about you? Are you able to manage your life perfectly and find fulfillment? Are you also able to plan your life after death? It is a certain fact that we are all travellers in this world; we know when we were born, but none of us knows exactly when we will depart. Where will you spend your next journey? Ah. You don't believe there is another life after this one? Are you certain? What if you find out after you died that there is one? Whatever your belief, my question to you is this: are you able to prepare for the next journey while still existing in the here and now? No one who is sane and knows for certain that an unexpected trip is coming would fail to ensure they had a suitcase packed with all their important documents, belongings, and plans.

In preparing for my transition from this world, I find answers in preparing to be with my perfect heavenly Father—God, our Abba, our higher power, however you want to name Him or Her.

Later in this book, we will discuss who we pray to. For now, though, you may be reading these lines and asking, "How can we be certain we will be with Him after death?" I am certain because I have chosen to believe that He is the way, the truth, and the life. Jesus told us, *"I am the way and the truth and the life. No one comes to the Father except through me."*

It is a choice, a question of my own free will. I can decide not to believe, but why would I take that risk? What if I were to die tonight and realized He was the way, the truth, and the life but I had missed the mark by choosing not to believe? Would I be able to come back to life and make it right? I know only one man who died and came back and His name is Jesus Christ. He told me that there is another life after this one. So I have chosen to believe him. Anyway, I don't have anything to lose and everything to gain in this life and the next. How about you?

Choosing to believe is the best option.

People often gamble and expect to win without knowing the results. They take that risk with their money. I'm encouraging you to gamble with your soul by choosing the way, the truth, and the life.

If you are a sceptic, realize that you won't lose anything by believing right now. You will live your best life by having a relationship with this wonderful God. And if it ends up being the right decision, you will win the jackpot.

Use your free will and choose wisely. Choose well.

You may wonder, as I once did, why we need to pray when the Word of God tells us that our heavenly Father already knows our needs before we ask, as it is written in Matthew 6:8: *"your Father knows what you need before you ask him."* But in the next verse, he tells us to pray for our needs. In 1 Thessalonians 5:17, God commands us to *"pray continually."*

The answer lies in the essence of a relationship, much like the one between a parent and a child. Parents often know what their children need and still desire the closeness that comes from their children coming to them, talking to them, asking them questions, and sharing their hearts.

> *Prayer is not just a commandment; it is an invitation to engage in a profound relationship with our Creator.*
> *It is therapeutic for the soul, offering a pathway to peace and comfort, knowing that our Father in heaven hears us when we pray.*

Prayer is not just a commandment; it is an invitation to engage in a profound relationship with our Creator. It is therapeutic for the soul, offering a pathway to peace and comfort, knowing that our Father in heaven hears us when we pray.

I find comfort in reading Mark 11:24: *"Therefore I tell you, whatever you ask for in prayer, believe that you have received it, and it will be yours."* This is a promise that our prayers will receive an answer. Whether it's a yes, no, or not now, the promise is certain. An answer will come. My God is truth, He cannot lie, and I choose to believe Him.

How about you?

WHY DO WE PRAY?

Let's unpack and answer this key question: why do we pray? I pray because I want to build a relationship with my perfect heavenly Father. I need someone trustworthy to whom I can go for conversation at all times—someone who created me, knows me, cares for me, loves me, and is able to help me at every level.

Don't we converse with other people in our lives? Conversation is a must in order to build, strengthen, and deepen any relationship. I see prayer as the same tool. It's a conversation with our God, our higher power, our Lord and Saviour. As Psalm 145:18 assures us, *"The Lord is near to all who call on him, to all who call on him in truth."* Who else can be available to me at all times? No one else is the King of Kings and Lord of Lords. No one else is omniscient, omnipresent, and omnipotent. So why wouldn't I take the time to speak to God? In the same way we speak to our loved ones and expect them to have relationships with us, we can speak to God through prayer.

> *Conversation is a must in order to build, strengthen, and deepen any relationship. I see prayer as the same tool. It's a conversation with our God, our higher power, our Lord and Saviour.*

In the book of Matthew, Jesus teaches us the value of sincere private prayer, emphasizing that God sees and rewards what is done in secret. Prayer is not about the quantity of our words, but the quality of our hearts. This is beautifully expressed in Matthew 6:5–8:

> And when you pray, do not be like the hypocrites, for they love to pray standing in the synagogues and on the street corners to be seen by others. Truly I tell you, they have received their reward in full. But when you

pray, go into your room, close the door and pray to your Father, who is unseen. Then your Father, who sees what is done in secret, will reward you. And when you pray, do not keep on babbling like pagans, for they think they will be heard because of their many words. Do not be like them, for your Father knows what you need before you ask him.

This passage is an invitation into intimacy with God, akin to the private conversations we cherish with our loved ones—those deep, heartfelt exchanges shared in the secrecy of our homes, bedrooms, or quiet spaces. In the same way, God invites us into a personal and intimate dialogue with Him—not to display our spirituality or impress others but to have a genuine, heart-to-heart conversation.

As human beings, we all long for intimacy. Our heavenly Father knows this and has provided a sacred place where He meets us in private. I encourage you to accept His invitation. Speak to Him openly, honestly, and with the sincerity of your heart, knowing that He hears and understands your every word in the secret place.

The word of God has taught me that prayer is our bold approach to God's throne, where we find mercy, grace, and the help we need in every situation, as noted in Hebrews 4:16: *"Let us then approach God's throne of grace with confidence, so that we may receive mercy and find grace to help us in our time of need."*

Just as we don't speak to our loved ones only once but continue to engage with them over time, our relationship with God thrives through constant communication. Prayer is the ongoing dialogue that deepens our connection with Him, aligning our hearts with His. God desires this continuous relationship with us, guiding us through every circumstance with joy, gratitude, and trust.

As 1 Thessalonians 5:16–18 beautifully reminds us, *"Rejoice always, pray continually, give thanks in all circumstances; for this is God's will for you in Christ Jesus."* Let this be an invitation for you to remain in constant prayer, nurturing your relationship with God just as you would with someone you deeply love.

In my journey, I have found that prayer replaces anxiety with God's peace, which transcends all understanding, guarding my hearts and minds. I still remember an author who wrote that if you can worry, you can pray. Because worry means pondering on issues, problems, and anything that might go wrong; prayer means pondering the promises of God and our faith in Him to help us get through trials and tribulations in a victorious way. My Lord God tells us in Philippians 4:6–7,

> *worry means pondering on issues, problems, and anything that might go wrong; prayer means pondering the promises of God and our faith in Him to help us get through trials and tribulations in a victorious way.*

> Do not be anxious about anything, but in every situation, by prayer and petition, with thanksgiving, present your requests to God. And the peace of God, which transcends all understanding, will guard your hearts and your minds in Christ Jesus.

But to reach this place of letting go of anxiety, I need to stay in prayer so His peace can guard my heart and minds.

How about you? Would you like to have that?

To Whom Do We Pray?

As mentioned earlier, knowing the person with whom we are having a conversation matters a lot. It shapes the way we address that person, establishes the level of our trust and expectation, and sets the stage for that conversation to happen.

Throughout my journey, I had to get to know the one to whom I have chosen to pray so I could establish a foundation for healthy conversation. Fortunately, the one I chose left a book for me to refer to—a book that is considered to be His Word, inspired many, many years ago. I have chosen to believe the Bible as the inspired Word of God. As it is written in *2 Timothy 3:16*, *"All Scripture is God-breathed and is useful for teaching, rebuking, correcting and training in righteousness."*

Once again, it is a choice. which book will be the compass of your life? What will you choose to trust as your guide?

If you haven't done so before, I invite you to take a look at the Bible. It is full of treasures. Believe me.

We all have various names that identify us—our first names, last names, and even nicknames—and we often attach deep meaning to them. It's no surprise that we feel hurt or offended when someone makes fun of our names.

For me, this significance is deeply personal. My youngest daughter's name was chosen to honour my late mother, whom I lost early in life. It's a name filled with love and meaning, as it also blends elements of both my mother's and my husband's mother's names.

However, when my husband shared our baby's name with one of his close family members, they laughed and ridiculed it, calling it the worst name they had ever heard. That deeply hurt me. It felt like a dismissal of the love and thoughtfulness behind the name. It also reminded me just how important names are—they represent identity, legacy, and the connections we cherish.

This is why it's crucial to understand to whom we speak and the significance behind their names. Even when answering a call from an unknown number, the first thing we usually ask is, "Who am I speaking to?" Names hold power. They define relationships and communicate respect and recognition. May we always treat names with the respect they deserve, honouring the stories and identities they represent.

Scripture also highlights the significance of names. For instance, God Himself reveals His names throughout the Bible, teaching us who He is through them. In Exodus 3:14, God introduces Himself to Moses as *"I AM WHO I AM"* (Exodus 3:14), declaring His eternal and unchanging nature. I love that name. My perfect heavenly Father names Himself I AM. To me, this represents His constant presence. Whether in the past, in the present, or in the future, He is.

Just as God's names reveal His character, the names we choose for our loved ones often carry deep meaning and tell a story.

Many scholars have come up with names for God, such as Yahweh (YHWH), which translates to "I am who I am" or "the self-existent one." Yahweh is God's personal and covenantal name, emphasizing His eternal existence and unchanging nature.

He is also known as *Adonai* (Lord, or Master), which signifies His authority and lordship over all creation; *El Shaddai* (God Almighty, or the all-sufficient one), which emphasizes God's power to sustain and provide for His people; *Elohim* (fullness of deity), which is used to describe His power and sovereignty as the Creator; *Emmanuel* (God with us), which signifies His presence among His people, fulfilled in the person of Jesus Christ; and *El Elyon* (the Most High God), which reflects His supreme sovereignty and exalted position above all other gods and powers.

Jehovah, a latinization of the Hebrew name Yəhōwā, which is itself a vocalization of YHWH, the tetragrammaton, is the proper name for the God of Israel in the Hebrew Bible. The Tetragrammaton is considered one of the seven names of God in Judaism and a form of God's name in Christianity.

There are several forms of Jehovah: *Jehovah Jireh* (the Lord will provide), which highlights God's provision, especially in times of need; *Jehovah Rapha* (the Lord who heals), which speaks to His power to heal physically, emotionally, and spiritually; *Jehovah Nissi* (the Lord is my banner), which represents His protection and leadership in battle; *Jehovah Shalom* (the Lord is peace), which underscores His provision of peace even in difficult times; *Jehovah Tsidkenu* (the Lord our righteousness), which reflects His role as the source of righteousness for His people; and *Jehovah Sabaoth* (the Lord of hosts), which portrays Him as the commander of the heavenly armies and angels, emphasizing His sovereignty and power.

These names all reveal different aspects of His nature and character.

But I have decided to give my God a nickname. Don't we give nicknames to our loved ones? In my country, nicknames are common. In the secular world, I've noticed that some cultures use nicknames more than real names, so much more, in fact, that people often forget people's real names.

Loved ones give nicknames to those they care about, whether it's something simple like "sweetheart" or "honey." These names let the person know they are precious. My dad's real name is Joseph Ambroise, but I cannot recall ever calling him that. I am very close to my dad, so using that name would surprise him and create distance. Instead I call him Papoute, a name which he loves. Whenever I call him that, it's as if he's willing to give me everything within his power.

So why wouldn't I give a dear nickname to my higher power? My sponsor, Naika, calls her God *Abba*. Romans 8:15 reflects this sentiment: *"The Spirit you received does not make you slaves, so that you live in fear again; rather, the Spirit you received brought about your adoption to sonship. And by him we cry, 'Abba, Father.'"*

I'm a little more complicated than that, so I call my Lord and Savior my perfect heavenly Father. It's a way to remind myself that He is not my earthly dad, who has fallen short so many times. Rather, He comes from heaven and is perfect. Because He is perfect, He is good, He is love, and He is powerful. He is everything that no one else will ever be for me and to me. He is my Father.

Given my relationship with my dad, it is very nurturing to embrace my God as a Father, and He is my God.

How about you? If you don't relate to a dad, what name could you use to make God, your higher power, with whom you choose to have a relationship, feel closer to you? Will you call Him Mother, Sister, King, Lord, Savior, Sweetie, Higher Power, Papa, Papi, or Abba? Take your pick. This is how personal a name needs to be in order for you to feel comfortable and at ease when talking to Him (or Her) in a place that is nurturing and loving.

Just as we have the right to nickname our God, He also has many names for us, and these names shape our identity in Him. We will explore them in the coming pages. It's crucial to get to know the names by which the one you choose to pray calls you. This sets the stage to see yourself from His

> *Just as we have the right to nickname our God, He also has many names for us, and these names shape our identity in Him.*

point of view, appreciating and loving yourself as you are—with all your flaws and shortcomings—because you are unique. No one in this whole universe has the same fingerprints as you, no matter how much they may physically resemble you.

According to Ephesians 2:10, *"[W]e are God's masterpiece. He has created us anew in Christ Jesus, so we can do the good things he planned for us long ago"* (NLT). Viewing yourself as God's masterpiece is important, as it glorifies the Father God who created you. No artist could fail to appreciate the value of His handiwork. The same is true for our God; if we treat ourselves as though we are nothing, we criticize He who created us and despise His work.

I have spent many years in that exact situation, complaining and murmuring in the desert over mistakes I've made and opportunities I've missed, believing that I'm not worthy. But you know what? A diamond that falls in the mud is still a diamond, no matter how dirty it is. The diamond needs to be picked up and cleaned so it can gleam again.

If you're reading this and find yourself in a stage of despising yourself, let me remind you that you are a piece of art. Whatever your hair type or skin colour, whatever the mud in which you find yourself in at this moment, I echo the words of David in Psalm 139:13–14: *"For you created my inmost being; you knit me together in my mother's womb. I praise you because I am fearfully and wonderfully made."*

God didn't just create us marvellously. He went further. Isaiah 49:16 tells us, *"See, I have engraved you on the palms of my hands; your walls are ever before me."* Aww! I feel loved.

My spouse uses his own pictures on his social media accounts, not mine. He also hasn't engraved my name on his hand. Yet my God, the Lord who created me, has done that, and it matters a lot to me, someone who has experienced rejection since I was a baby. I need acceptance, I need connection, I need to feel appreciated and loved. This has brought me to a point of accepting myself despite my flaws so I can love myself. Because if I am not able to love myself, I cannot love my neighbour. The Word of my God is clear: *"For the entire law is fulfilled in keeping this one command: 'Love your neighbor as yourself'"* (Galatians 5:14).

Before I can love my neighbour, I need to love myself first. Then I can love them as myself. But if I despise myself—whether for the way I look, where I come from, the mistakes I've made, or because people have rejected me and I have started rejecting myself—I will be unable to love others.

The journey of learning to love myself in a healthy way has taken me years, but it's been worth every step. If you're on a similar path, I invite you to start today. Look in the mirror and say, "I love myself. I love my life." Repeat it every day. Then give yourself a big hug—wrap your arms around your shoulders tightly and hold on.

Self-love is the foundation of self-care, and it's where true healing and the ability to love others begins. You are worth it.

The Names God Calls Us

Speaking of names, do you know what God calls me, what He calls my brothers and sisters who have been adopted into His family? He also has great names for you and me, which is further proof of how much He loves us and encourages us to love ourselves so we can love others.

The Bible, which I have chosen to believe as the Word of God, contains some of the names and titles that God, my Perfect heavenly Father, uses to describe you and me.

We are God's creation. God acknowledges us as His creation. Psalm 100:3 says, *"Know that the Lord, He is God; it is He who has made us, and not we ourselves; we are His people and the sheep of His pasture"* (NKJV). This verse emphasizes that we have been made by Him and belong to Him. I feel blessed, encouraged, and honoured to be created in the image of the Creator of the world.

But being created in His image means more than bearing a physical resemblance to Him. Our connection to His nature is much deeper.

While we may not share God's divine form, our ability to think, create, and express love mirrors Him. Our capacity for emotion, reason, and creativity reflects His character. Just as He is the ultimate Creator, we too have been given the ability to create and shape the world around us.

Moreover, our resemblance to God extends to our inner beings—our capacity for love, justice, mercy, and compassion. These characteristics are rooted in God's nature and are part of who we are because we have been made in His likeness. When we show kindness to others, forgive those who wrong us, and seek justice, we reflect the image of God in our daily lives. Our spiritual longing, our quest for meaning and purpose, and our ability to connect with Him through prayer and worship all point to the divine imprint within us.

In every aspect of our beings—physically, emotionally, and spiritually—we bear the marks of our Creator. This realization fills me with a profound sense of purpose and belonging. Knowing that I have been made in God's image inspires me to live in a way that reflects His love, wisdom, and holiness to the world around me, which in turn encourages me to speak with Him at all times.

God has chosen to adopt us. God adopts us into His family, calling us His sons and daughters, indicating a close and loving relationship. As we read in 2 Corinthians 6:18, *"I will be a Father to you, and you shall be My sons and daughters, says the Lord Almighty"* (NKJV).

I really like this spirit of adoption. When a family adopts children, they cannot unadopt them or give them back. The same is true when we give birth to children. No matter how our relationship with them turns out, they will always be our children and we will always be their parents. So it is for those who have chosen God to be their Father; we are adopted as His daughters and sons and share the same rank as Jesus Christ, His beloved Son.

When God calls us His sons and daughters, it reflects His deep commitment to us. In the same way that a biological parent cannot sever the bond with their child, God's adoption of us is irrevocable. This relationship isn't just a formal or legal connection; it is a deep, loving, and eternal bond. God's love for us as His children is unwavering, and He delights in us as any loving parent would.

I read in 1 John 3:2, *"Dear friends, now we are children of God, and what we will be has not yet been made known."* How does that you make feel as a child of the Most High? It is nurturing for me. I don't feel like a stranger. I feel precious, loved, and grateful that through the Holy

Spirit I have received the spirit of adoption. This verse emphasizes the closeness of our relationship with God. He is not just a distant deity but our loving Father. This is why I can feel confident and at ease in coming to Him as much as I wish.

We are God's children. By believing in Jesus, by receiving Him, I have been given the right to become a child of God: *"But as many as received Him, to them He gave the right to become children of God, to those who believe in His name…"* (John 1:12, NKJV) This verse highlights the fact that our status as sons and daughters is a privilege granted by our faith in Christ.

I also find Galatians 4:6–7 to be very encouraging:

> And because you are sons, God has sent forth the Spirit of His Son into your hearts, crying out, "Abba, Father!" Therefore you are no longer a slave but a son, and if a son, then an heir of God through Christ. (NKJV)

Are there any children who wouldn't want to inherit from their fathers? I certainly do, especially since my father is a King. Being a son or daughter of God means that we are His heirs, sharing in the inheritance that comes through Christ. This passage underscores our secure and honoured place in God's family. Being elevated to the rank of Jesus Christ fills me with joy.

You might ask, who is Jesus Christ? That is a subject for another time. But in summary, one may say that He was the greatest man to ever live. He was both the Son of God as well as God Himself, one hundred percent God and one hundred percent human. Hebrews 1:3 says, *"The Son is the radiance of God's glory and the exact representation of his being, sustaining all things by his powerful word."* Jesus is described as the exact representation of God's being, implying His divine nature.

This is the person with whom I am being compared. Isn't it wonderful? That's amazing! God has already promised me His inheritance, which I receive through Christ in this world. My inheritance is also awaiting my coming in the next life.

This triggers my willingness to speak to Him as often as possible.

Our identity as God's sons and daughters is central to our faith. It means that we are loved, cherished, and valued by the Creator of the universe. Just as Jesus is the Son of God, we too are His children, sharing in His love, promises, and eternal kingdom. This adoption is a profound act of grace, and it assures us that we belong to Him forever. Therefore, I feel compelled to remain connected to Him, speaking with my perfect heavenly Father at all times.

God calls us His friends. In addition to a daughter, God also calls me a friend. As a mother of three, including young adult children, I deeply understand what it means to be a friend to my kids. As they grow and embark on their own lives, physical distance can create a void. We long for the regular conversation and connection we once had. My husband and I are grateful for the children who stay in touch, sending notes, messages, or emails—sharing pieces of their lives, asking for advice, or simply joking around.

This connection, this friendship, mirrors the relationship God desires with us. It goes beyond the parent-child bond, inviting us into a two-way relationship in which intimacy and communication flourish.

Friendship with God is characterized by an open exchange. He not only reveals His heart to us but invites us to share our hearts with Him. In prayer and communion, we can speak freely, knowing that He listens with understanding and compassion.

I often find myself joking with God. Sometimes when I'm alone and something funny happens, I laugh and tell Him, "You've got a good sense of humour, don't You?" We talk and laugh together in the car, while doing laundry, while I'm cooking, or even while exercising. We play and joke around just as friends do. And while it might seem silly to an outsider, who cares? This is what friendship is about, enjoying each other's company. This is the kind of relationship God wants to build with us, on in which we are His best friends.

In Exodus 33:11, we read, *"So the Lord spoke to Moses face to face, as a man speaks to his friend" (NKJV).* The friendship between God and Moses illustrates the depth of communication and intimacy God desires with us. He wants to converse with us openly and honestly, just as friends do.

Moreover, Jesus's friendship with us is eternal. Unlike human friendships, which may fade over time, Jesus promises to never leave or forsake us. He is a constant companion in our lives, guiding, comforting, and standing by us through all circumstances. Many people have come into my life who I hoped would stay forever, but they walked away at the first opportunity. I've learned that people come into our lives for a reason, and a season. Very few stay for a lifetime. And that's okay. Imagine if you had kept all your friends from over the years. Where would you find the time and energy to maintain those relationships?

It's natural for people to come and go, but you and I know that we need some to stay forever. God is the one friend we can be certain will stay forever, no matter what we face—not only in this life but in the life to come. I need that. How about you?

Being called a friend of Jesus is a profound honour. It means we're loved, valued, and trusted by the King of Kings. It also challenges us to live up to this friendship by being faithful, loyal, and true to Him, just as He is to us. John 15:15 tells us,

> No longer do I call you servants, for a servant does not know what his master is doing; but I have called you friends, for all things that I heard from My Father I have made known to you. (NKJV)

This verse reminds us that Jesus calls us friends, signifying an intimate relationship wherein He shares His heart and plans with us. This transforms our relationships with Him. We are more like friends than servants. Unlike a master who keeps his servants in the dark, Jesus invites us into His confidence, revealing to us the mysteries of God's kingdom and divine will.

In the ancient world, a servant was expected to obey without question, often without understanding the reasons behind the master's commands. Jesus does not treat us like servants. Instead He elevates us to the status of friends. We are privy to His thoughts, intentions, and desires. This friendship is marked by trust, openness, and mutual love.

Jesus's friendship with us isn't casual or superficial. It is a deep, abiding connection rooted in love and sacrifice. He laid down His life for us, the greatest demonstration of love a friend can show. This is seen in John 15:13: *"Greater love has no one than this: to lay down one's life for one's friends."* This act of selflessness underscores the profound bond we share with Him.

My perfect heavenly Father highlights the importance of friendship in Proverbs 18:24: *"A man who has friends must himself be friendly, but there is a friend who sticks closer than a brother"* (NKJV). This verse highlights the unique nature of true friendship, which can sometimes be even more loyal and intimate than a familial bond. Jesus is that friend who sticks closer than a brother. He is always present, always faithful. I long to talk at all times with such a friend.

Abraham's relationship with God is described as a friendship, emphasizing the fact that faith and trust in God lead to a close, personal connection with Him. My perfect heavenly Father states in James 2:23: *"And the Scripture was fulfilled which says, 'Abraham believed God, and it was accounted to him for righteousness.' And he was called the friend of God"* (NKJV).

Just as Abraham was called God's friend, we too are invited into that same relationship through faith in Christ. So God is my bestie and I feel compelled to talk to Him at all times and share everything with him.

How about you?

We are the apple of God's eye. God also calls us the apple of His eye. How beautiful that is! Deuteronomy 32:10 says, *"He found him in a desert land and in the wasteland, a howling wilderness; He encircled him, He instructed him, He kept him as the apple of His eye"* (NKJV). This verse reflects God's treatment of Israel as the apple of His eye, providing guidance, protection, attention, and care even in the most desolate and dangerous places. It underscores God's unfailing commitment to those He loves, even when they are in the midst of adversity.

Zechariah 2:8 adds, *"For thus says the Lord of hosts: 'He sent Me after glory, to the nations which plunder you; for he who touches you touches the apple of His eye'"* (NKJV). Here, God warns that anyone who harms His people is essentially attacking the most sensitive and cherished part of

Him. This powerfully illustrates how closely God identifies with His people and how precious they are to Him. It showcases the deep value He places on His people.

This expression, apple of His eye, is a vivid illustration of how precious and cherished we are in the eyes of God. It refers to the pupil, the most sensitive and protected part of the eye. Just as the pupil is guarded and shielded from harm, so too does God protect and care for those who are dear to Him.

In ancient literature, including the Bible, this phrase is often used to describe something or someone that is highly valued and closely guarded. By asking God to keep us as the apple of His eye, the psalmist invoked the deep, protective love God has for His people. It signifies that we are not just loved, but we are treasured, guarded, and constantly in His watchful care.

God's love for us is so profound that He views us as invaluable, just as we instinctively protect our own eyes. He is constant vigilant over us, ensuring that we are shielded from harm, both physically and spiritually. His care for us is personal and intimate, reflecting His deep affection and concern for our well-being. Just as we protect our eyes from even the smallest threat, God is keenly aware of every detail of our lives and actively involved in safeguarding us.

This is a beautiful reminder of our worth in His sight. It speaks to the tender love and care He has for us individually. We are not just one among many; we are uniquely loved and valued by the Creator of the universe. He watches over us with a careful eye, ensuring that nothing can separate us from His love.

The psalmist wrote in Psalm 17:8, *"Keep me as the apple of your eye; hide me in the shadow of your wings"* (NKJV). This paints a picture of God as a protective parent, shielding us from danger, much like a mother bird protects her chicks. This dual imagery emphasizes both our value to God and the lengths to which He goes to ensure our safety and well-being.

God calls us beloved. Romans 9:25 states, quoting the prophet Hosea, *"I will call them 'my people,' who are not my people; and I will call her 'my loved one' who is not my loved one"* (NKJV). To me, this highlights

God's transformative love, taking those who were once outsiders and bringing them into His fold as His beloved. It underscores the inclusivity of God's love and the grace extended to all who come to Him.

The term beloved carries profound significance in the context of our relationship with God. To be called beloved is to be deeply loved, cherished, and valued. It reflects the intense and personal affection God has for each of His children. The word is a powerful affirmation of our identity in Christ. We are not just followers or servants; we are beloved, held in the highest regard by our Creator.

This word is used throughout the New Testament to describe those who are in Christ, emphasizing the special bond that exists between God and His people. This love isn't based on our merits or actions; it is an expression of God's grace and unchanging nature. Being beloved means that we are recipients of God's unwavering love, a love that is constant and eternal.

In calling us beloved, God also reminds us of our worth and value. The world may often make us feel unworthy or insignificant, but in God's eyes we are precious and irreplaceable. His love for us is so great that He sent His only Son to die for our sins, demonstrating the ultimate act of love. As beloved children of God, we are called to live in the light of this love, embracing our identity as those who are deeply loved and cherished by the Creator of the universe.

In Ephesians 1:6, we read, *"to the praise of the glory of His grace, by which He made us accepted in the Beloved"* (NKJV). In this verse, *"the Beloved"* refers to Jesus Christ, emphasizing that through Christ we are accepted and loved by God. Our beloved status is directly tied to our relationship with Jesus, who mediates God's love to us.

Being God's beloved also calls us to reflect His love in our interactions with others. We are deeply loved, and thus we are called to love others with the same intensity and commitment. This love is meant to be transformative, shaping our character and guiding our actions.

Our belovedness is foundational to our faith, a reminder that we are not defined by our past, failures, or opinions of others. Instead we are defined by the love of God, which is perfect, unconditional, and everlasting. In this love, we find our true identity and purpose, knowing that we are forever cherished by our heavenly Father.

A royal priesthood, a holy nation, a chosen people. Other names by which God calls us are found in 1 Peter 2:9: *"But you are a chosen generation, a royal priesthood, a holy nation, His own special people, that you may proclaim the praises of Him who called you out of darkness into His marvelous light"* (NKJV).

Isn't it amazing that we have been chosen by God to be His special people, set apart for His purposes? Being described as a chosen people highlights the special status believers hold in God's eyes. This verse captures the essence of our identity as God's chosen ones, selected by Him to fulfill a unique purpose in His divine plan. To be chosen means that God has set us apart not because of our worthiness but because of His grace and sovereign will.

The concept of being chosen by God is deeply rooted in the history of Israel. He chose the nation of Israel to be His special people, set apart to reflect His glory to the other nations. In the New Testament, this closeness is extended to all believers in Christ, who come to be considered part of God's chosen people regardless of their ethnic or cultural background.

This chosen status comes with both privilege and responsibility. As God's chosen people, we are called to be a royal priesthood, serving as mediators between God and the world, offering spiritual sacrifices and proclaiming His praises. We are also called to be a holy nation, set apart from the world in our conduct and values, reflecting the holiness of God in every aspect of our lives.

I am encouraged by Deuteronomy 7:6, which states, *"For you are a holy people to the Lord your God; the Lord your God has chosen you to be a people for Himself, a special treasure above all the peoples on the face of the earth"* (NKJV). Thi echoes the theme of choosiness, emphasizing that God's people are His special treasure, set apart from the rest of the world. It serves as a reminder that our identity as chosen people is not based on our merit but on God's love and purpose.

This verse from the Old Testament echoes John 15:16: *"You did not choose Me, but I chose you and appointed you that you should go and bear fruit, and that your fruit should remain, that whatever you ask the Father in My name He may give you"* (NKJV). Jesus emphasizes that choosing us is an act of His will, not ours. We have been chosen with a purpose—to bear fruit that glorifies God. This reinforces the idea that being chosen is both a privilege and a calling to fulfill the mission for which God has created us.

Our identity as God's chosen people is meant to inspire confidence and purpose. Knowing that we have been chosen by God should give us assurance that our lives have meaning and significance in His plan. It also calls us to live in a manner worthy of this calling, reflecting God's character and proclaiming His goodness to the world.

Being chosen also implies that we are part of a larger community, a holy nation that transcends geographical and cultural boundaries. We are united with believers across the globe in a shared identity and mission, bound together by the love and purpose of God. This global community of believers is a testament to God's diverse and inclusive kingdom in which all are welcome and valued.

In recognizing our status as God's chosen people, we are reminded of His faithfulness and the incredible privilege of being part of His redemptive work in the world. We have been chosen not just for our own sake, but to be a light to others, to proclaim the praises of He who called us out of darkness and into His marvellous light.

We are God's heirs. As believers and children of God, we are not only part of His family but also beneficiaries of His promises. Romans 8:17 states, *"and if children, then heirs—heirs of God and joint heirs with Christ, if indeed we suffer with Him, that we may also be glorified together"* (NKJV). As children of God, we are also heirs to His promises, sharing in His glory.

This verse speaks to a profound reality—that our relationship with God extends beyond mere kinship. It includes the inheritance of all that God has promised. To be an heir means to receive a share of the estate, and in this spiritual context it means inheriting the blessings and promises that God has prepared for His people.

Being an heir of God signifies that we have been given access to His spiritual riches. This inheritance includes eternal life, the gifts of the

Holy Spirit, and the blessings of His presence and guidance in this life. It is a mark of our privileged position in God's family, affirming our value and the depth of God's love for us.

Moreover, being joint heirs with Christ reveals that our inheritance is shared with Jesus. This is an incredible honour, since Christ is the Son of God and heir to the Father's promises. Our shared inheritance with Christ means that we are included in the glory and blessings He receives. It underscores the unity and relationship we have with Jesus, who is both our Savior and fellow heir.

The passage also notes that suffering is part of this journey. To be glorified with Christ, we must first share in His suffering. This doesn't mean that suffering is the goal, but rather that it is part of the process of becoming more like Christ and preparing for the fullness of our inheritance. Through trials and challenges, we are being refined and strengthened, aligning ourselves with the character of Christ and preparing us for the glory that is to come.

In Galatians 4:7, we read, *"Therefore you are no longer a slave but a son, and if a son, then an heir of God through Christ"* (NKJV). This reinforces the idea that as children of God, we are heirs. Our status as heirs is a direct result of our relationship with Christ, who has made it possible for us to inherit God's promises.

Ephesians 1:11 states, *"In Him also we have obtained an inheritance, being predestined according to the purpose of Him who works all things according to the counsel of His will..."* (NKJV) Our inheritance is part of God's eternal plan and purpose. Our place in God's family and the inheritance we receive are not random but align with His divine will.

Understanding our status as heirs shapes how we view ourselves. It assures us of our security in God and motivates us to live in a manner that honours our calling. It also produces in us hope and encouragement, knowing that a glorious inheritance awaits us despite the current difficulties. It sets the stages for me to converse with the king at all times because I can come to Him in a loving relationship.

God calls us saints. I must confess that when I've read this word, "saints," I've laughed. We all know what it means: someone who is perfect, even holy. I personally believed that to be a saint, a person needed to be canonized by the church. Such a person also couldn't be alive anymore.

I couldn't understand that God, despite my shortcomings, could call me a saint. But it is a fact. We are called saints, meaning that we have been set apart and made holy through our relationship with God. In Romans 1:7, my perfect heavenly Father inspired these words: *"To all who are in Rome, beloved of God, called to be saints: Grace to you and peace from God our Father and the Lord Jesus Christ"* (NKJV).

I am not in Rome, but I am a believer in the same way as those Romans. That term, a saint, refers to those who have been set apart for God and made holy through their relationship with Him. It signifies a special status given to believers who are called to reflect His holiness and character. Being called a saint emphasizes my identity in Christ; I haven't just been forgiven but transformed and set apart for God's purposes.

The concept of sainthood in Scripture isn't limited to a select few. It includes all believers. Through Christ, we are all called to lives of holiness and righteousness. This calling means that we are to live according to God's standards, reflecting His character in our daily lives.

Being a saint also involves a process of sanctification wherein we are continually made more like Christ. This process includes growing in faith, developing godly character, and living out our calling with integrity and devotion. It is a call to embrace our new identity in Christ and live in a way that honours Him.

My perfect heavenly Father shows that the calling to be saints is universal among all believers. As we read in 1 Corinthians 1:2,

> To the church of God which is at Corinth, to those who are sanctified in Christ Jesus, called to be saints, with all who in every place call on the name of Jesus Christ our Lord, both theirs and ours… (NKJV)

Being a saint is not about personal achievement but about being sanctified in Christ and living out that sanctification in our relationship with God and others.

Ephesians 1:4 says that *"just as He chose us in Him before the foundation of the world, that we should be holy and without blame before Him in love"* (NKJV). My calling to be a saint is part of God's eternal plan. It underscores that we have been chosen for lives of holiness, reflecting His love and character in our interactions and conduct.

Recognizing ourselves as saints helps us to understand our role and responsibilities in the body of Christ. It calls us to a higher standard of living, reflecting the love, grace, and holiness of God in our daily lives. It also offers assurance and confidence, knowing that we are set apart and valued.

Embracing our identity as saints helps us to live with purpose, aligning our actions with God's will and contributing to His work in the world. It reminds us that our lives have a divine purpose and that we are empowered by the Holy Spirit to live out our calling as children of God. It encourages me to speak to Him in the place of sanctification He asks me to embrace.

We have been made anew. In Christ, we are made new, leaving behind our old selves and embracing a new identity in Him, as written in 2 Corinthians 5:17, *"Therefore, if anyone is in Christ, he is a new creation; old things have passed away; behold, all things have become new"* (NKJV).

For many, the concept of new identity can be difficult to comprehend. When I moved from my home country to build a life somewhere new, I came to better appreciate the concept and impact of identity in our lives. If you have more than one citizenship, you know what it is to become a citizen of a new country, one in which you have to learn many new things and leave behind your former self.

In French, they say, *"Partir c'est mourir un peu."* In other words, "Travelling is like dying a little bit." Changing citizenship can feel this way. In Christ, we are made anew and called to embrace our new identity, one which captures the transformative power of being in Christ. As a new creation, our identity is fundamentally changed. The "old things" that have passed away refer to our former way of life, characterized by sin, brokenness, and separation from God. This transformation isn't just a superficial change but a deep, inner renewal that affects every aspect of our being.

In Christ, we are given a fresh start—a new identity that reflects our relationship with Him. The new in us is a reflection of the newness of life Christ offers. This new creation is characterized by a new heart, a new mind, and a new purpose. We are no longer defined by our past mistakes or failures but by our new identity in Christ.

The transformation is both a present reality and future hope. While we are being renewed daily, we also look forward to the complete restoration that will be realized in eternity. This new creation is a call to live in alignment with our new identity, embracing the values, behaviours, and purposes that reflect our relationship with Christ.

In Christ, what truly matters is our identity as a new creation in Christ rather than any external religious practice or tradition. As Galatians 6:15 states, *"For in Christ Jesus neither circumcision nor uncircumcision avails anything, but a new creation"* (NKJV).

I am so grateful that my identity in Christ transcends cultural or ritualistic differences.

As new creations, we are called to live in righteousness and holiness, reflecting the character of God in our daily lives, emphasizing the practical outworking of our new identity, as is written in Ephesians 4:24: *"and that you put on the new man which was created according to God, in true righteousness and holiness"* (NKJV).

Embracing our identity as a new creation means rejecting the old ways and fully accepting the new life Christ offers. This encourages us to live with a renewed mindset, pursuing growth in faith and aligning our actions with our new identity. It also provides us hope and motivation, causing us to know that we are continually being transformed into the likeness of Christ.

We are God's temple. My perfect heavenly Father even writes about my body, which He describes in His Word as the temple wherein His own spirit dwells, as written in 1 Corinthians 3:16: *"Do you not know that you are the temple of God and that the Spirit of God dwells in you?"* (NKJV)

This verse reveals the profound truth that our bodies are not just physical entities but sacred spaces wherein God's Spirit resides. The concept of being a temple of the Holy Spirit underscores the immense value and sanctity of our bodies as vessels for God's presence.

In the Old Testament, the temple was that place where God's presence dwelled, and it was regarded as holy and set apart. In the New Testament, this concept is expanded to include every believer. As temples of the Holy Spirit, we carry the presence of God within us, signifying that our lives are to be lived in reverence and honour to Him.

This understanding of our identity has significant implications for how we live. It calls us to treat our bodies with respect, to avoid behaviours that would defile them, and to embrace a lifestyle that reflects the holiness of God's Spirit within us. It also emphasizes that our spiritual relationship with God is intimate and personal, as He dwells within us and guides us from within.

Many verses reiterate the truth that our bodies are temples of the Holy Spirit. 1 Corinthians 6:19 states, *"Or do you not know that your body is the temple of the Holy Spirit who is in you, whom you have from God, and you are not your own?"* (NKJV)

I am very grateful that I am not my own but belong to my perfect heavenly Father, which highlights my responsibility to honour Him through my life and choices.

I read in 2 Corinthians 6:16,

> And what agreement has the temple of God with idols? For you are the temple of the living God. As God has said: "I will dwell in them and walk among them. I will be their God, and they shall be My people." (NKJV)

This calls us to separate ourselves from any influences that would compromise the holiness of God's presence within us. Recognizing ourselves as temples of the Holy Spirit transforms our perspective on our bodies, our relationship with Him through prayers, and our daily lives. It prompts us to live in a way that honours God's presence within us, fostering a lifestyle of purity, integrity, and devotion. This understanding deepens our relationship with God, encouraging us to seek His guidance and reflect His character in all aspects of our lives, conversing with Him at all times.

We are the light of the world. Jesus calls His followers the light of the world, a powerful metaphor that highlights our role in reflecting His truth and love. Matthew 5:14 says, *"You are the light of the world. A city that is set on a hill cannot be hidden"* (NKJV).

Light symbolizes guidance, purity, and visibility, contrasting with darkness, which represents ignorance, sin, and hiddenness. As the light of the world, we are meant to illuminate the path for others by embodying the teachings and character of Christ. Just as a city on a hill stands out and cannot be hidden, our lives should visibly reflect God's presence, influencing those around us and pointing them towards Him.

Our role as light involves several aspects:

- Guidance. We are to provide direction and clarity in moral and spiritual matters, helping others find their way in the midst of confusion or darkness.
- Visibility. We are to live in such a way that our faith is evident to others, demonstrating the transformative power of Christ in our lives.
- Purity. We reflect the purity and righteousness of God, which contrasts with the moral decay and corruption in the world.

Being a light means actively engaging in acts of love, justice, and compassion, allowing us to make a positive difference in our communities and the world.

We read in John 8:12, *"Then Jesus spoke to them again, saying, 'I am the light of the world. He who follows Me shall not walk in darkness, but have the light of life'"* (NKJV). Jesus identifies Himself as the ultimate light, and by following Him we receive the light of life, enabling us to be effective lights to others.

As a result, I am compelled to live a blameless and innocent life that helps me shine amidst a corrupt world, reflecting God's truth and love, as stated in Philippians 2:15: *"that you may become blameless and harm-*

less, children of God without fault in the midst of a crooked and perverse generation, among whom you shine as lights in the world..." (NKJV)

Embracing our identity as the light of the world involves an active and intentional pursuit of living out our faith in a way that influences others. It challenges us to be aware of our impact on those around us and strive to make a difference by reflecting Christ's light in all we do.

I am compelled to be the light of the world by reflecting God's truth and love to the world around me. But how would I succeed if I don't converse with the one who has appointed me to be directed, led and encouraged?

We are the salt of the world. Jesus uses the metaphor of salt to describe our role in the world. We read in Matthew 5:13, *"You are the salt of the earth. But if the salt loses its saltiness, how can it be made salty again? It is no longer good for anything, except to be thrown out and trampled underfoot."*

Salt serves several key purposes:

- Preservation. Just as salt preserves food from decay, Christians are called to preserve their moral and spiritual integrity in society, counteracting corruption and promoting righteousness.
- Flavour. Salt enhances the taste of food. Similarly, our presence should add value and bring out the best in the world around us, making life more flavourful and meaningful.
- Healing. Salt has healing properties, and we are called to be agents of healing and restoration, bringing comfort and reconciliation where there is brokenness.

This warning about salt losing its saltiness serves as a caution against becoming ineffective or irrelevant in our role. It highlights the importance of maintaining our distinctiveness and influence as followers of Christ.

Therefore, I am called to maintain my effectiveness and impact as the salt of the earth. Mark 9:50 says, *"Salt is good, but if the salt loses flavor, how will you season it? Have salt in yourselves, and have peace with one another"* (NKJV). This verse connects the metaphor to living in harmony and peace.

My perfect heavenly Father is saying that my interactions should be thoughtful and impactful, reflecting the saltiness of grace and wisdom, which is what I am called to do as stated in Colossians 4:6: *"Let your speech always be with grace, seasoned with salt, that you may know how you ought to answer each one"* (NKJV). Being the salt of the earth involves actively preserving, enhancing, and healing others through our actions and words. It challenges us to remain effective in our role by living out our faith authentically and purposefully, thereby making a positive impact on the world around us.

These names and titles reflect the multifaceted relationship God has with His children, portraying us as loved, chosen, and valuable in His sight.

> *These names and titles reflect the multifaceted relationship God has with His children, portraying us as loved, chosen, and valuable in His sight.*

Wouldn't you feel encouraged, empowered, and even compelled to converse with God as often as possible, given the closeness of your relationship with Him? I don't know your love languages, but I agree with Gary Chapman that we all have a predominant one.[1] The universal love language we all share is that we feel good when we are loved and appreciated. This feeling nurtures and deepens our relationships.

If I choose God and surrender my life to His will, and if He chooses to give me all these beautiful nicknames, I must converse with Him. I need to get to know Him in a deeper, more intimate way, to pour out my heart, share my struggles, and grow in my relationship with Him.

Just as He has called me many great names that shape my identity, I can also nickname my perfect heavenly Father in a way that translates my relationship with Him.

Do you agree that getting to know the people you converse with deepens your relationship with them? Knowing what they think about

---

[1] Gary Chapman, *The Five Love Languages: How to Express Heartfelt Commitment to Your Mate* (Chicago, IL: Northfield Publishing, 1992).

you and appreciating their love for you sets the stage for healthy conversation. The same is true when it comes to the one you choose as your Lord and Savior.

When Do We Pray?
I don't know about you, but I pray all the time. That might seem like an exaggeration, so let me confess that it wasn't always this way. I wasn't raised in a family that prayed regularly. When I started going to school, prayer was just part of the routine, much like honouring the flag. Those recitations became something we did out of habit—maybe in the morning, before bed, before a meal, or during church services. Saying these prayers was never a way of living; they felt more like a ritual than a way to meaningfully connect with God.

As I began to walk with the Lord and better understood what prayer truly is, I naturally figured out when to pray.

The answer is that a relationship with God is similar to our relationships with other people. Think about it. When do we talk to those we care about? At all times, whenever the need arises. When we first meet someone, we speak to them a little. Over time, we speak more often. Conversations are a way to get to know each other, share our lives, and encourage one another.

So prayer is more than just a routine or habit. It's a conversation—a two-way exchange in which we both speak and listen. It's about building a relationship with God just as we would with family, friends, and colleagues. We converse in many forms—spoken words, gestures, or even in writing—but the key is that these interactions need to happen regularly for the relationship to grow.

Speaking of written communication, do you remember the old days when people wrote love letters to one another? In more recent years, this tradition has changed. We now send ecards, emails, texts, and social media messages. Regardless of the form, though, it is a fact that we communicate with the ones we love.

I love to write, and so I often write my prayers. If it's easier for you to communicate to God in written form, you can do that. There is no right or wrong way. Whatever method we use, it should be personal. That way, it will deepen our connection and relationship with our God.

So I encourage you to ask yourself this key question. Is your God a distant, impersonal deity whom you should fear, or is He part of your inner circle, like a family member, close friend, or loved one? Your answer to this question will set the stage for your prayer life.

I have chosen my God, the one who calls Himself I AM. I call Him perfect heavenly Father and long to know Him more. Because I want to deepen my relationship with Him, I need to talk to Him as often as possible. Through my relationship with my heavenly Father, His mind, heart, and character are revealed to me in the Word, the Bible. I also see Him in the people He created, including my spouse, children, pastor, and brothers and sisters. I even see Him in my dreams or through my conscience. My heavenly Father is the Creator of the universe and His characteristics of being omniscient, omnipotent, and omnipresent are foundational to understanding His nature; they encourage me to come to Him knowing that He is the only one who has it all, knows it all, and can be everywhere simultaneously.

Let's briefly define these terms and explore how the Word of God supports them. These characteristics compel me to come into His presence, stay there, and clean my own personal temple as He continues to live within me so I can grow in looking more like Him every day.

A proverb states that we resemble those we spend most of our time with. This is why I want to spend the bulk of my time in this life with my perfect heavenly Father: because I long to resemble Him in every way possible.

The Lord I choose to abide with, yield and surrender to, is omniscient (all-knowing), omnipotent (all-powerful) and omnipresent (present everywhere).

Omniscience. God's omniscience means that He has complete and perfect knowledge of all things. He knows everything—past, present, and future—and is aware of all thoughts, actions, and events. I am confident about Him because of these passages:

> You have searched me, Lord, and you know me. You know when I sit and when I rise; you perceive my thoughts from afar. You discern my going out and my lying down; you are familiar with all my ways. Before a word is on my tongue you, Lord, know it completely. (Psalm 139:1–4)
>
> If our hearts condemn us, we know that God is greater than our hearts, and he knows everything. (1 John 3:20)
>
> Remember the former things, those of long ago; I am God, and there is no other; I am God, and there is none like me. I make known the end from the beginning, from ancient times, what is still to come. I say, "My purpose will stand, and I will do all that I please." (Isaiah 46:9–10)

While I am limited, my God is all-knowing. I long to talk to Him as often as possible, seeking to gain bits of His knowledge.

If you know a very powerful figure who knows a lot and invites you to talk to him whenever you want, would you hesitate? Would you be reluctant to seize this opportunity? Should not the same be true for your Lord and God? Who wouldn't want to grow in knowledge, especially from the source of all knowledge?

Omnipotence. I read of God's omnipotence throughout those scriptures that refers to His unlimited power. He can do anything consistent with His nature and will. When I read the following verses, I grow in confidence that there is nothing too difficult for God to accomplish.

> Ah, Sovereign Lord, you have made the heavens and the earth by your great power and outstretched arm. Nothing is too hard for you. (Jeremiah 32:17)

> Jesus looked at them and said, "With man this is impossible, but with God all things are possible." (Matthew 19:26)

> Then I heard what sounded like a great multitude, like the roar of rushing waters and like loud peals of thunder, shouting:
> "Hallelujah! For our Lord God Almighty reigns. (Revelation 19:6)

Given that my God is all-powerful, I need to seek His strength through constant conversation. Who wouldn't want to draw from the ultimate source of power? I would want that. How about you?

Omnipresence. God's omnipresence means that He is present everywhere at the same time. There is no place in the universe where He is not present. I know of his omnipresence because I have chosen to believe in his Word, which states,

> Where can I go from your Spirit? Where can I flee from your presence? If I go up to the heavens, you are there; if I make my bed in the depths, you are there. If I rise on the wings of the dawn, if I settle on the far side of the sea, even there your hand will guide me, your right hand will hold me fast. (Psalm 139:7–10)

> "Am I only a God nearby," declares the Lord, "and not a God far away? Who can hide in secret places so that I cannot see them?" declares the Lord. "Do not I fill heaven and earth?" (Jeremiah 23:23–24)

> And surely I am with you always, to the very end of the age. (Matthew 28:20)

My God is everywhere while I am limited to one place at a time. I long to connect with Him constantly, acknowledging that He is with me always, no matter where I am, confident that He knows my next step. He knows where I'm going and what's going to happen since He is simultaneously in the past, present, and future. Who wouldn't want to feel the presence of their Creator everywhere they go, knowing that He is going before us and will prepare the way?

I want to make sure that I connect to God, intimately, through prayer. By engaging in continual conversation, I come to understand Him more deeply and grow in my faith.

Prayer isn't just a routine; it's the lifeblood of my relationship with God. As I talk to Him, I grow, learn, and become more aligned with His will for my life.

This is why it's easy for me to pray all the time. It's not out of obligation, but out of a deep desire to know the one who knows me, strengthens me, and is always with me. I pray because I want to stay connected to my heavenly Father, who loves me more than I could ever imagine.

> *I also have a set prayer time. It's like having an appointment or date with a loved one.*

I also have a set prayer time. It's like having an appointment or date with a loved one.

Lovers don't just spend time talking. They also set aside special moments to go on dates. One of the reasons that a marriage fails is that the couple becomes too accustomed to each other. They often stop going on dates. Marriage is intended to be a partnership which produces oneness, yet many couples neglect to connect meaningfully to discuss the state of their relationship, their goals, and other issues impacting them. As a result, disagreements and assumptions arise, turning conversations into disputes.

In any partnership or collaboration, regular discussions are essential in order to align, plan, and resolve issues—and the same principle applies to your relationship with your higher power. Without intentional communication and connection, the stage is set for misunderstanding and deception.

The same is true when it comes to our relationship with our higher power. Therefore, I establish a daily time and duration to be alone with

Him without distraction. This echoes Matthew 6:6, which encourages us to go to our rooms and close the door to pray: *"But you, when you pray, go into your room, and when you have shut your door, pray to your Father who is in the secret place; and your Father who sees in secret will reward you openly"* (NKJV). During this personal appointment, I usually put music. I sometimes sing, dance, and worship. I come into His presence to give Him all the praise, all the honour, and all the glory. I sometimes also cry silently, or loudly, depending on how I feel. I read scriptures before, during, and after these prayer times to seek guidance, hearing what the Lord wants to communicate to me.

When I was young, I used to go on spiritual retreats. I loved those retreats more than anything. I enjoy being silent in nature where everything is quiet. There is no chatting, and no noise, only an opportunity to connect to the Lord.

Because we live in a busy and noisy world, it's refreshing to the soul to quiet the constant sound so we can hear the voice of God within us. This calls to mind the prophet Elijah's encounter with God in 1 Kings 19:11–13:

> The Lord said, "Go out and stand on the mountain in the presence of the Lord, for the Lord is about to pass by."
>
> Then a great and powerful wind tore the mountains apart and shattered the rocks before the Lord, but the Lord was not in the wind. After the wind there was an earthquake, but the Lord was not in the earthquake. After the earthquake came a fire, but the Lord was not in the fire. And after the fire came a gentle whisper. When Elijah heard it, he pulled his cloak over his face and went out and stood at the mouth of the cave.
>
> Then a voice said to him, "What are you doing here, Elijah?"

God's showed Himself to Elijah in a gentle whisper. In this same way, there are times when we need quiet time to hear God.

Therefore, besides being connected to Him at all times in our hearts and minds, we must also go on dates with Him. We can plan a weekend retreat to go out into nature to connect with Him on a regular basis. This should be part of one's ritual to get refreshed and deepen one's connection and relationship with Him.

Praying at all times gives me room to pray without even letting people know that I'm praying. It also echoes the call of my perfect heavenly Father to not show off with my prayers, like the Pharisees written about in Matthew 6:5:

> And when you pray, you shall not be like the hypocrites. For they love to pray standing in the synagogues and on the corners of the streets, that they may be seen by men. Assuredly, I say to you, they have their reward. (NKJV)

So I ask you, dear reader—when do you pray, and when do you feel compelled to pray? It's your decision. But one thing I know—your relationship with your God will remain shallow if you don't converse with Him. Prayer is a conversation; it's the lifeblood of your relationship with God. Without it, your connection will suffer from spiritual anaemia and wither away—that is, if you don't continually stay in touch, conversing and meditating with Him to gain encouragement, help, and strength.

The Lord's Prayer, given by Jesus, is a model that balances reverence for God with personal petitions. It begins by acknowledging His holiness and then turns to our own needs, teaching us the priorities of prayer. If you feel stuck in how to start, you can find your answer in Matthew 6:9–13:

> This, then, is how you should pray: "Our Father in heaven, hallowed be your name, your kingdom come, your will be done, on earth as it is in heaven. Give us today our daily bread. And forgive us our debts, as we also have forgiven our debtors. And lead us not into temptation, but deliver us from the evil one."

From there, you can add your own elements to personalize your prayer time.

Now that I've gone over the why, who, and when of prayer, it's time to explore the question of how one should pray.

Part Two
PERSONAL PRAYERS

I invite you to join me on a journey of deep personal connection with God. These prayers are born from my own spiritual walk, in which I've sought to align every aspect of my life with God's will.

The Bible reminds us in Matthew 6:33, *"But seek first his kingdom and his righteousness, and all these things will be given to you as well."*

As I share these prayers, my hope is that they will inspire you to seek God with all your heart, knowing that He cares deeply about every detail of our lives.

Breath Prayers

For those who pray regularly, you will agree that we sometimes speak *breath prayers*, like "Oh my God, help me" or "Oh Lord, I can't take it anymore" or "Please God, have mercy." Do you know that these too are considered prayers?

God, whom I choose to serve, does not respond to my prayers because they are long, short, thoughtful, or well-crafted. This is why, through the habit of praying for many years, I have embraced some short breath prayers.

One short breath prayer I have embraced uses the acrostic PRAY.

P is for praise. The psalmist often praises the Lord and encourages everything that has breath to praise the Lord (Psalm 150:6). We praise God for who He is; it is a way to worship the giver of all things instead of focusing on the gifts.

For instance, parents love when their kids appreciate their gifts, but they cherish even more when their kids appreciate them beyond what they can provide. No one likes to feel used for what they bring to the table. That's why, when the brook dries up, we often know deep down that we may never see that person or child again.

The same is true with our relationship with God. Praising Him first and foremost is a way to show that we love Him with all our hearts, minds, and souls. We praise Him through songs of worship, counting His blessings, and simply acknowledging who He is.

Think about how you approach a friend or loved one. When you call or go on a date, you don't immediately ask them for something. Instead you greet them warmly, compliment their appearance, or engage in light-hearted conversation. Only later, as the connection deepens, might you share a need or request—unless it's strictly a transactional meeting, where the focus is on making an exchange.

For a relationship to thrive over time, it cannot always be transactional. If it is, the relationship may not survive. The same principle applies to our conversations with God. If we only approach Him when we want something, we risk rendering the relationship shallow and unsustainable.

In my personal journey, I praise Him with the letters of the alphabet, with each letter standing for a quality I admire about Him. For example, A can stand for *absolute* or *advocate*, B for *beautiful* or *benevolent*, and C for *caring, comforter,* or *counsellor*.

How about you? Find the best way that fits you to praise and worship your Lord and Savior because He is worthy of praise. In the meantime, let's embrace Psalm 150:1–5:

> Praise the Lord! Praise God in his sanctuary; praise him in his mighty heavens! Praise him for his mighty deeds; praise him according to his excellent greatness! Praise him with trumpet sound; praise him with lute and harp! Praise him with tambourine and dance; praise him with strings and pipe! Praise him with sounding cymbals; praise him with loud clashing cymbals! (ESV)

R is for repent. Why is it so important to repent when we pray? The short answer is that repentance clears the way. It involves changing the mind and heart regarding a past action or attitude and turning away from it in favour of a more righteous path. It involves acknowledging and regretting a wrongdoing while committing to avoid similar actions in the future.

What I like about this definition is that it is twofold: when we repent, we sincerely regret what we did and commit to not repeating it. Repentance is not a quick "Sorry," followed by the same thing over and over.

When I transitioned from my upbringing to a new culture, I was astonished at how people would say sorry without any real attitude of regret, let alone making a commitment not to hurt others again. Without those two things, our repentance avails nothing. Acts 3:19 makes this clear: *"Repent, therefore, and turn back, that your sins may be blotted out..."* (ESV)

Another reason to repent is that prayer is an offering to God. We offer Him our praise and worship, taking time to pour out our hearts before Him. And because it is an offering, Matthew 5:23–24 encourages,

> Therefore, if you are offering your gift at the altar and there remember that your brother or sister has something against you, leave your gift there in front of the altar. First go and be reconciled to them; then come and offer your gift.

Sometimes it isn't easy, or even possible, to make things right with someone. Perhaps the person is unreachable, has already passed, or going to them would do more harm than good.

Therefore, I invite you to make a list of all the people you have harmed and be willing to make amends to them all. This is step eight in the twelve-step process which we will discuss later in this book. By writing out these names, as well as what we did to them, we take the step of regretting our action.

In the following step, we are to make direct amends to such people when possible, except when doing so would harm or injure them or others.

In cases where it is impossible, make a commitment before God not to repeat what you have done. And if the person isn't around, commit to not do to others what you did to them. This demonstrates that you are truly sorry, that you've learned your lesson and are ready to commit to making lasting changes.

It is also very important to forgive those who have wronged us. I usually combine repentance with praying for the people who have hurt me, asking God to soften my heart so I can choose to forgive them. Forgiveness means relinquishing my desire to get even, removing all bitterness and unforgiveness, as these poisons will harm me rather than those against whom I hold them.

Moreover, forgiving them opens the door for God to forgive my own shortcomings. Matthew 6:14–15 makes it clear: *"For if you forgive other people when they sin against you, your heavenly Father will also forgive you. But if you do not forgive others their sins, your Father will not forgive your sins."*

So, my friend, I encourage you to promptly repent and forgive, clearing the way for your offering to God to be fruitful.

A is for ask. I'm sure I don't need to elaborate too much here, as our prayer request—in other words, our ask—often outweighs everything else. We have so much to ask God!

My focus is to encourage you to increase your faith when you ask. In my journey with God, I have realized that many times my ask is shaky, as if I'm asking without really expecting anything. It's a way to avoid disappointment.

This might work in our relationships with others, since people are fallible, but we should avoid this with God. God is not like man; He is trustworthy and we ought to have faith. Besides, as Hebrews 11:6 says, *"And without faith it is impossible to please God, because anyone who comes to him must believe that he exists and that he rewards those who earnestly seek him."*

When we ask God, we should be confident that we will receive an answer. Yes, I wrote "an answer". It may not be exactly what we asked for.

God has three possible answers when we ask Him: yes, no, or not now. His answers come with love, for He knows what is best for us at any moment. He won't give us something we ask for right away if He knows we aren't ready to receive it. Maybe He has something better in store for us.

The Word of God is full of verses that encourage us to ask with faith. Matthew 21:22 says, *"And whatever things you ask in prayer, believing, you will receive"* (NKJV). What I love about that verse is that sometimes we don't receive because we don't have enough faith; we are double-minded, not even sure if we want what we are asking for. Sometimes we even doubt whether God can give it to us. We might think He can give it to others but feel we don't deserve it. So it's important to adopt your attitude as a child of God, an heir, and believe that God will give you what is best. But you must ask and believe.

James 4:3 says, *"You ask and do not receive because you ask amiss, that you may spend it on your pleasures"* (NKJV). This is profound. It dives into the reasons behind our requests.

For example, if I ask God for a new car because my friend bought a new car, I have motivation issues. Am I motivated to have a car to help me fulfill my mission effectively, or do I simply want to show off to the people around me? This can result in a no answer because the reasons behind my request aren't right. So check your motivations when you ask.

On the other hand, the Word of God makes it clear that an attitude of faith will ensure that whatever we ask is done for us. Jesus reassured us in John 14:13–14: *"And whatever you ask in My name, that I will do, that the Father may be glorified in the Son. If you ask anything in My name, I will do it"* (NKJV). And Matthew 7:7 encourages us, *"Ask, and it will be given to you; seek, and you will find; knock, and it will be opened to you"* (NKJV).

My friend, let's cultivate an attitude of being motivated by our love for God, bearing confidence that He will provide an answer according to His will.

Y is for yield. Yielding, in a biblical context, means to submit or surrender one's will to the authority and guidance of God. The word yield derives from the Old English *gieldan*, originally meant "to pay" or "surrender to."[2] In the spiritual sense, yielding implies a voluntary act of giving up control, allowing God's will to take precedence over our own.

At first glance, obeying and yielding might seem like the same thing, but they hold distinct meanings relating to our relationship with God.

Obeying involves following God's commands and instructions, acting according to His will. It's about doing what God has asked us to do, often through His Word, with a focus on our actions and behaviour.

Yielding, on the other hand, goes a step further. Yielding is about the posture of our heart and mind. It's not just about doing what God asks but also about surrendering our own will, desires, and plans to His will. It's a deeper level of submission wherein we allow God to have full control, even when His plans differ from our own or when His will seems challenging.

Yielding to God's means recognizing that His plan is superior to ours, trusting Him even when His commands seem difficult or contrary to our desires. It involves surrendering our preferences, plans, and desires in favour of God's purposes. This requires humility, faith, and a deep trust in God's goodness and wisdom.

We see this in the life of Mary. In Luke 1:38, she yields to God's will when she responds to the angel Gabriel by saying, *"I am the Lord's servant... May your word to me be fulfilled."*

Have you ever taken the time to think about what it would have been like for a young unmarried girl in that kind of society to find out she would become pregnant? Even her fiancé Joseph planned to leave her quietly, not wanting to expose her to public disgrace.

At that time, Mary could have been stoned to death for being pregnant out of wedlock. Yet she was confident that the angel had brought

---

[2] "Yield," *Online Etymology Dictionary*. Date of access: December 16, 2024 (https://www.etymonline.com/word/yield).

a word from the Lord. So she yielded to God's will without bargaining or complaining, trusting that He would make a way where there seemed to be no way. Despite the potential risks and societal implications, Mary surrendered her life to God's plan.

In your breath prayer, after you've given praise, repented, and asked, it's time to surrender to the outcome. Surrender whether the answer is no, not now, or yes, knowing and believing that your God has great things in store for you. He knows what's best for you and will certainly give you that best.

Another quick breath prayer I say in the morning when I wake up, as soon as I open my eyes, is to say good morning to God and worship Him for the new day He has made. I ask Him to help me to rejoice and be glad in it. I then commit my day to Him by asking Him to help me in whatever I say, do, or think, so that my actions will align with the values of His kingdom, ensuring that I won't regret anything tomorrow. I want to be proud of today, reminding myself to take it easy, one day at a time, and not stretch myself too thin. I put my confidence entirely in my perfect heavenly Father.

I encourage you to find what works best for you and to deepen your relationship with God.

TACOS

Another acrostic prayer I wish to include is one I first heard from Pastor Vlad Savchuk, whose ministry has deeply impacted my spiritual journey. It follows the word *tacos*.

T is for thanksgiving. Gratitude is a cornerstone of faith, reminding us to appreciate God's blessings in our lives. As Psalm 100:4 encourages us, *"Enter his gates with thanksgiving and his courts with praise; give thanks to him and praise his name."* Similarly, 1 Thessalonians 5:18 reminds us to *"give thanks in all circumstances; for this is God's will for you in Christ Jesus."*

Thanksgiving isn't just a response to blessings; it's a way of life that acknowledges God's goodness, even in difficult times. As we thank Him, we open our hearts to receive even more of His grace and blessings.

A is for adoration. Adoration invites us to worship God for who He is, beyond what He does. It allows us to express love and reverence for God, our Creator and Sustainer. Psalm 95:6 says, *"Come, let us bow down in worship, let us kneel before the Lord our Maker."*

Through adoration, we exalt God's greatness and proclaim His holiness. Revelation 4:11 declares, *"You are worthy, our Lord and God, to receive glory and honor and power, for you created all things..."* Let your adoration flow from a heart captivated by God's majesty.

C is for confession. Confession invites us to bring our sins and shortcomings before God, seeking His forgiveness and grace. It is an act of humility that acknowledges our dependence on His mercy. We are reassured in 1 John 1:9, *"If we confess our sins, he is faithful and just and will forgive us our sins and purify us from all unrighteousness."*

This step also includes forgiving those who have wronged us, reflecting God's forgiveness toward us. Proverbs 28:13 reminds us, *"Whoever conceals their sins does not prosper, but the one who confesses and renounces them finds mercy."* Confession clears the path for forging a deeper connection with God.

O is for others. Here we are encouraged to intercede for the people in our lives. Scripture calls us to lift up our family, friends, and community in prayer. As 1 Timothy 2:1 says, *"I urge, then, first of all, that petitions, prayers, intercession and thanksgiving be made for all people..."* As we pray for others, we fulfill our role as spiritual advocates, trusting God to work in their lives. James 5:16 affirms, *"The prayer of a righteous person is powerful and effective."*

S is for self. Finally, we are to bring our own personal needs and desires to God. Philippians 4:6 encourages us, *"Do not be anxious about anything, but in every situation, by prayer and petition, with thanksgiving, present your requests to God."* Whether we need wisdom, healing, or guidance, we can trust that God hears and answers according to His perfect will. Psalm 62:8 says, *"Trust in him at all times, you people; pour out your hearts to him, for God is our refuge."*

The TACOS prayer model provides a comprehensive approach to prayer, guiding us through gratitude, worship, confession, intercession, and personal petitions. As you embrace this framework, may it deepen your relationship with God and enrich your spiritual journey.

Prayer Essentials for Self

Next we will dive into my prayer essentials, which are lengthier than breath prayers or TACOS prayers and serve as guide during the times I set aside to speak to my Father on a regular basis.

There are twenty of them in total, but in this section of the book I will begin by focusing on the ten that are personal in nature. In the next part of the book, I'll walk through the ten that focus instead on praying for others.

1. Love God first, prioritizing Him in every aspect. During my personal prayer time, I earnestly pray that God will give me the strength to love Him with all my heart, mind, and strength, as this is the first and greatest commandment. This commandment is found in several places in Scripture: *"You shall love the Lord your God with all your heart, with all your soul, and with all your strength"* (Deuteronomy 6:5, NKJV).

This verse from the Old Testament is part of the Shema, a daily prayer in Jewish tradition. It calls for total devotion to God, encompassing every aspect of our being—our emotions (heart), spiritual essence (soul), and physical energy (strength). For believers, it signifies that our love for God should be complete and undivided. God wants one hundred percent of our love and devotion, whereas the enemy of our soul wants just a tiny percentage, a foothold to destroy us. According to John 10:10, *"The thief comes only to steal and kill and destroy; I have come that they may have life, and have it to the full."* Therefore, give God one hundred percent.

In Matthew 22:37–38, Jesus declares, *"'You shall love the Lord your God with all your heart, with all your soul, and with all your mind.' This is the first and great commandment"* (NKJV). Here, He emphasizes importance of loving God with one's whole being, starting with the heart.

Dr. Anita Phillips, in her transformative book *The Garden Within*, beautifully illustrates the concept of the heart as a garden. She explains that the soil of our hearts is where every seed—whether of love, faith, or healing—takes root and grows. The quality of this soil determines the fruits we produce in our lives, impacting not only our spiritual health but also our emotional and relational well-being.[3]

This insight has profoundly shaped my understanding of how vital it is to cultivate a healthy, receptive heart in my walk with God.

Jesus's inclusion of the mind in this commandment highlights the intellectual dimension of loving God. It reminds us that our thoughts, reasoning, and understanding should align with His will and purposes. Loving God with our minds means engaging in purposeful reflection, studying His Word, and allowing His truth to shape our thinking.

Together, these aspects—heart, soul, and mind—form a holistic approach to living in complete devotion to God, nurturing both the inner garden of our hearts and the clarity of our minds.

In Mark 12:30, Jesus reiterates this commandment, adding strength, which encompasses our physical capabilities: *"'And you shall love the Lord your God with all your heart, with all your soul, with all your mind, and with all your strength.' This is the first commandment"* (NKJV). This teaches us that our love for God should manifest in our actions, as well as in our emotions and thoughts. Every part of our lives should reflect our devotion to Him.

Loving God with all our heart, soul, mind, and strength means that our devotion to Him is complete and all-encompassing. There should be no part of our lives at which He is not the centre. If there is, the enemy will use it to gain a foothold in our lives to lead us into sin.

This commandment is the foundation of our relationship with God. It sets the tone for how we live, make decisions, and interact with others. Without this love, our faith lacks the true connection and purpose God desires for us.

When we love God with all our being, we draw strength from Him. This love fuels our perseverance, guides our decisions, and gives us the courage to face challenges. Through this love, we find the strength to follow God's commandments and live out His will in our lives.

This prayer and reflection can be a powerful reminder of the central place that our love for God should take in our lives as believers. Loving

---

[3] Anita Phillips, *The Garden Within: Where the War with Your Emotions Ends and Your Most Beautiful Life Begins* (Charlotte, NC: T.D. Jakes Ministries, 2022).

God with all my heart, mind, and soul, when translated into action, gives God first place in my life.

Author and preacher Rick Warren has used the acrostic FIRST to invite God to take first place in his life. I use it daily in my own prayer time, asking God to give me a heart that causes me to love him with all my heart, mind, and soul.

This acrostic is a practical way to prioritize God in the various aspects of our lives. It's a concept that resonates with biblical principles of putting God first in everything. In my prayer time, I invite God to be first in each of these areas.

F is for finances. Will you agree that money is central to everything in life, whether you have a lot, too much, not enough, or none at all? We all use money. We need it to sustain ourselves and take care of our loved ones.

Yet many of us have been raised to view money in unhealthy ways, either as something to chase obsessively or as something inherently evil.

It's unclear why Christians in some cultures are often portrayed as needy and poor, but the Bible never says that money itself is evil. As 1 Timothy 6:10 states, *"For the love of money is a root of all kinds of evil, for which some have strayed from the faith in their greediness, and pierced themselves through with many sorrows"* (NKJV). This verse emphasizes that it's not money that is evil, but the love of money. When money becomes an idol or obsession, it can lead to sinful behaviour, including greed, dishonesty, and even turning away from God. The pursuit of wealth can lead to spiritual ruin and emotional suffering.

Our view of money often leads to scarcity, chasing wealth, or pretending we don't need money at all. However, the Bible teaches about generosity: *"I have shown you in every way, by laboring like this, that you must support the weak. And remember the words of the Lord Jesus, that He said, 'It is more blessed to give than to receive'"* (Acts 20:35, NKJV).

The apostle Paul reminds us that giving is more blessed than receiving. This encourages a mindset of using money to help others and bless those in need. How can we give if we don't have money? We ought to pray for our finances, commit them to God, and make sure we are reflecting our kingship as princes and princesses.

I pray that God will bless me abundantly so I can give abundantly. I pray the same over your lives as well.

Friends, I encourage you to focus your prayers on multiplying the resources God has given you rather than complaining about not having enough. I have learned to ask God to bless my finances, reminding myself that I am the daughter of the almighty King. Even if I don't yet have my inheritance, I am a princess; therefore, I ask my father to be involved in my income and to help me use the talents He has given me to create wealth rather than hiding it away like the third servant in the parable of the talents.

In Matthew 25:14–30, a master entrusts three servants with varying amounts of talents, a form of currency in ancient times. The first two servants invest their talents and double their money while the third buries his out of fear and does nothing with it. When the master returns, he praises the first two servants for their faithfulness and resourcefulness but rebukes and punishes the third servant for his inaction.

God has entrusted each of us with resources, abilities, and opportunities—and He expects us to be good stewards. This involves not only preserving what we have but also actively growing these resources. It is about stewardship and responsibility.

The parable also teaches about entrepreneurship and investment. The servants who invested their talents and returned a profit can be seen as models for entrepreneurship. The parable suggests there is value in taking calculated risks and making wise investments to multiply what has been entrusted to us. This can be interpreted as a divine endorsement to use our talents and resources to build wealth, create value, and contribute to the flourishing of others.

The third servant's decision to bury his talent was met with severe criticism. It is unacceptable to be fearful and lazy in managing what God has given us. The parable encourages believers to take action and make the most of their opportunities.

While the parable has a spiritual dimension, emphasizing the importance of using spiritual gifts for the kingdom of God, it also has practical applications. It encourages diligence, creativity, and a desire to grow and improve in our work, finances, and personal development. We will all be held accountable for how we use the resources and opportunities God has given us. The expectation is not merely that we will maintain what we have but increase it, fulfilling God's purpose for our lives.

Praying for God to be first in my finances means asking Him to guide me in developing an entrepreneurial mindset, seeking opportunities to build wealth, and ensuring that my finances serve His purposes rather than controlling me. God has never commanded me to be poor or labelled money as evil; instead He has warned that the love of money is the root of all evil. Therefore, I pray for His help to never love money, revenue, or any income He has entrusted to me more than I love Him.

Everything I have is a gift from Him. He is the One who gives me life, health, and opportunities to earn income. When I give back to Him, I am not offering something that is inherently mine but rather a portion of what He has already provided. It is an acknowledgment of His provision and sovereignty.

Being faithful through tithes and offerings is my way of showing gratitude, obedience, and trust in Him. As Proverbs 3:9–10 reminds us, *"Honor the Lord with your wealth, with the firstfruits of all your crops; then your barns will be filled to overflowing, and your vats will brim over with new wine."* Giving back to Him first isn't just a spiritual practice but a divine mandate—for without Him we have nothing.

By prioritizing God in my financial life, I affirm my trust in His provision and invite Him to continue blessing me as I strive to use His gifts for His glory.

I also pray for discipline in my finances so I won't spend more than I have. In fact, I must be content with what I have. It's not about how much I make but how much I save.

Before I knew the Lord, shopping was a huge problem for me. I spent more than I earned. A scarcity mindset propelled me to buy things I thought I would need. Later, I realized that all it did was max out my credit card. I sometimes had to resell my purchases at a loss to pay off my debt. It was such an unhealthy way to live.

Since I started placing God first in my finances, He has given me discipline. I now pray about my purchases, setting a budget for what I truly need instead of what I merely want. I am disciplined with money to the extent that I can walk into a store, buy just what I need, and leave without succumbing to other temptations. We live in a world of hot deals, but remember that the same deal you saw yesterday will come around again.

If you need financial discipline, surrender your finances, income, and expenses to God. He will bless you abundantly. Given the significant role that finances play in our lives, I encourage you to pray about your finances.

Agur, a lesser-known figure in the Bible, is credited with the sayings in Proverbs 30. He acknowledges his own limitations and seeks wisdom from God. In this particular passage, he makes a humble request for two things before he dies. The first is for honesty and integrity. He asks God to keep falsehood and lies away from him. The second request is for balanced provision, neither too much nor too little. We read in Proverbs 30:7–9:

> Two things I request of You (deprive me not before I die): remove falsehood and lies far from me; give me neither poverty nor riches—feed me with the food allotted to me; lest I be full and deny You, and say, "Who is the Lord?" Or lest I be poor and steal, and profane the name of my God. (NKJV)

This passage shows the wisdom in seeking a balanced life. It acknowledges the need for provision while warning against the dangers of both poverty and wealth.

Agur's prayer reflects a deep understanding of human nature and the pitfalls associated with extreme wealth or poverty. He recognizes that having too much might lead him to forget God and become self-sufficient and prideful, questioning, "Who is the Lord?" Conversely, having too little might tempt him to steal, thereby dishonouring God.

Agur's prayer is a plea for contentment and reliance on God. He desires just enough to meet his needs, enabling him to live a life that honours God without falling into the spiritual pitfalls of either extreme wealth or dire poverty. It is a powerful reminder of the importance of contentment and the dangers of greed and desperation.

I also pray Agur's prayer, asking God to grant me enough wealth so I can have abundance to share with those in need and use that wealth for the advancement of His kingdom, giving Him all the praise, honour, and glory. I encourage you to pray for financial discipline and an entrepreneurial mindset regarding your finances.

The Bible provides clear guidance on how believers should relate to money, emphasizing the importance of a balanced perspective. While money itself is not inherently evil, the love of money can lead to harmful behaviour and spiritual danger. The Bible teaches that money is a necessary part of life but must be handled with care and wisdom. Believers are encouraged to avoid the love of money, which can lead to evil, and instead focus on contentment, generosity, and trusting in God's provision. Money should be seen as a resource to be used for good rather than an end in itself.

In asking God to be first in my finances, I also pray that He will give me the heart to sow generously through my tithes and offerings. As 2 Corinthians 9:6–7 says:

> But this I say: He who sows sparingly will also reap sparingly, and he who sows bountifully will also reap bountifully. So let each one give as he purposes in his heart, not grudgingly or of necessity; for God loves a cheerful giver. (NKJV)

Putting God in first place in my finances means setting aside the portion I've dedicated to Him right away when my income comes in. This practice reminds me that the ability to earn that money is a gift from God. I am alive by His grace; not only am I alive, but I am also emotionally, physically, and mentally healthy, with the strength, courage, and intelligence to work. I cheerfully give back for the advancement of His kingdom.

The Bible encourages generosity, teaching that those who give generously will also receive blessings. The attitude with which one gives is important, for God values cheerful and willing giving.

This attitude has blessed me throughout my life. Though I was born into a very poor family, God has provided for me beyond measure since I've come to know and walk with Him, often in miraculous ways. I am the first college graduate on my mother's side, and I have been able to support my children through education to invest, create, and be spiritually comfortable—not by my strength alone, but by the grace of God who has blessed my finances.

I invite you to engage in your conversations with God. If you do, you will experience abundant blessings in this area.

I is for interests. During my personal prayer time, I ask God to help me put Him at the centre of my interests. Our interests, what we are passionate about and captures our attention, are powerful indicators of what truly matters to us. When we place God at the centre of our interests, we align our passion with His purpose and find deeper fulfillment. The Bible encourages us to prioritize God in all aspects of our lives, including our interests.

In Matthew 6:33, Jesus instructs us: *"But seek first the kingdom of God and His righteousness, and all these things shall be added to you"* (NKJV). Jesus Himself provides an example of prioritizing God's interests above all else.

This verse underscores the importance of making God our primary focus. When we seek His kingdom and righteousness above all else, our interests will naturally align with His will. He will provide for our needs and desires according to His plan. When we prioritize God's kingdom and righteousness, our earthly needs and concerns will be taken care of. Our interests should not be limited to our personal desires but should be directed towards God's work and purposes.

Another example can be seen in the life of the apostle Paul, who was transformed by his encounter with Christ. In Philippians 3:8, he wrote,

> Yet indeed I also count all things loss for the excellence of the knowledge of Christ Jesus my Lord, for whom I have suffered the loss of all things, and count them as rubbish, that I may gain Christ... (NKJV)

Paul's shift in interests from worldly achievements to knowing Christ demonstrates the transformative power of putting God at the centre. His new interests were rooted in his relationship with Jesus, leading him to a life of purpose and fulfillment.

When we make God the focus of our interests, we find that our passions and pursuits become more meaningful. We view our talents, hobbies, and ambitions through the lens of God's purpose, seeking to use them for His glory and the benefit of others.

Our interests often reflect what is truly important to us. In the context of our spiritual lives, aligning our interests with God's will is essential. The Bible provides clear guidance on making God the centre of our interests and passions.

In Colossians 3:2, we are instructed, "Set *your minds on things above, not on earthly things.*" This underscores the fact that God desires our interests to align with His will and purposes. By focusing on heavenly things, we ensure that our passions and pursuits are rooted in our relationship with Him, leading us to live in accordance with His plans for us.

Another relevant story is found in Luke 10:38-42, where Martha and Mary welcome Jesus into their home. While Martha is distracted by the demands of serving, Mary chooses to sit at Jesus's feet and listen to His teachings. Jesus commends Mary for choosing the *"good part"* (Luke 10:42, NKJV) that would not be taken away from her. Martha's focus is on doing things for Jesus, but Jesus desires us to simply be with Him.

This story serves as a powerful reminder for myself when I find that I'm taking on too much or becoming overwhelmed. I often tell myself, "I am not a human doing, but a human being." This simple truth encourages me to slow down, rest in His presence, and prioritize being over doing.

Our primary focus should be on nurturing our relationship with Jesus rather than being consumed by worldly distractions. As Psalm 37:4 advises, *"Delight yourself also in the Lord, and He shall give you the desires of your heart"* (NKJV). When our interests and desires align with God's will, He fulfills our deepest longings in ways that honour Him and bring lasting blessings.

Our interests should be centred on nurturing our relationship with Jesus rather than being overwhelmed by worldly concerns. When our interests and desires align with God's will, He fulfills our deepest longings in ways that honour Him and bless us.

Incorporating God into our interests involves more than just setting aside time for spiritual activities. It means integrating His values into every aspect of our lives, ensuring that our passions, hobbies, and pursuits reflect our commitment to Him.

This is why during my prayer time I ask God to help me put Him in first place in my interests. As I pray for God to be first in my interests, I seek His guidance to align my passions with His will, making His kingdom my primary focus.

I encourage you to reflect on your own interests and consider how they align with your relationship with God. Pray for guidance in aligning your passions with His will, trusting that He will direct your paths and fulfill your deepest desires according to His perfect plan.

Evaluate your own interests and passions and consider how you can centre them around God's purpose for your life. By doing so, you will find a greater sense of fulfillment, knowing that your interests contribute to His glory and align with His eternal plans.

I pray that God will be at the centre of my interests on a daily basis and invite you to do the same.

R is for relationships. Relationships are fundamental to our lives, encompassing our connections with family, friends, and colleagues. How about we place God in first position on this list? I ask that God will give me the grace to always remember that He is my first connection, the cornerstone of my relationship before people, places, and things.

The Bible provides clear guidance on how we should approach our relationships, emphasizing the importance of centring them around God's love and principles.

Consider the story of Ruth and Naomi. Ruth's loyalty and commitment to her mother-in-law demonstrates a relationship grounded in love and faithfulness. Ruth's decision to stay with Naomi and support her, even when it meant leaving her own homeland, exemplifies how relationships centerd around God's love can lead to blessings and provision.

Another powerful example is found in the relationship between David and Jonathan, as described in 1 Samuel 18:1: *"Now when he had finished speaking to Saul, the soul of Jonathan was knit to the soul of David, and Jonathan loved him as his own soul"* (NKJV). Their friendship, characterized by deep loyalty and mutual support, reflected a relationship rooted in God's love and faithfulness.

One of the key aspects of making God first in our relationships is turning to Him before anyone or anything else. Instead of seeking validation or solutions from people, places, or things, we should first seek God's guidance and wisdom. Proverbs 3:5–6 reminds us, *"Trust in the Lord with all your heart, and lean not on your own understanding; in all your ways acknowledge Him, and He shall direct your paths"* (NKJV). By prioritizing God in our relationships, we ensure that our connections are grounded in His truth and love.

I have been used by people who pretended to be in my inner circle. They were my friends but then rejected me after they got what they wanted. I know what it's like to feel alone in the middle of a crowd. Relationship can be very challenging and sometimes we feel as though we would be better off alone.

However, we know that nobody is an island. We need others.

When we face challenges in our relationships, it's essential to pray and seek God's guidance rather than relying solely on our own efforts or advice from others. Psalm 37:5 says, *"Commit your way to the Lord; trust in him and he will do this."* When we place our trust in God, He will help us navigate our relationships with grace and wisdom.

By putting God first in our relationships, we allow His love to guide our interactions, leading to healthier, more fulfilling connections. This involves seeking His wisdom in resolving conflicts, offering forgiveness, and showing grace to others.

It also involves the discernment to differentiate the people who come to our lives for a season, for a reason, or for a lifetime. It gives us a sense of detachment when someone walks away; we can peacefully let them go knowing that God is the only person who will never reject us. He is the same yesterday, today and tomorrow.

As I pray for God to be first in my relationships, I ask Him to help me reflect His love in all my interactions, strengthening my bonds with others through His guidance. I invite God to be the glue that holds my relationships together, trusting that He, who knows all our hearts, understands the purpose of each connection and its season in my life. I seek His wisdom and discernment to evaluate my relationships, ensuring they are healthy and aligned with His will.

I encourage you to consider how you can centre your relationships on God, making Him the foundation and highest priority in your interactions and decisions. By doing so, you will experience deeper, more meaningful connections that honour God and radiate His love to those around you.

S is for schedules. Our daily schedules often reflect what we prioritize. Many years ago, I started saying good morning to God as soon as I open my eyes in the morning. I then offer a short prayer before getting out of bed. I make space in my agenda for prayer throughout the day. To me, it matters that I give first place to the one who can redeem time in my agenda.

> *I make space in my agenda for prayer throughout the day. To me, it matters that I give first place to the one who can redeem time in my agenda.*

As followers of Christ, it's crucial to put God first in our schedules, acknowledging Him from the moment we wake up. By saying good morning as we open our eyes, we establish first contact and build our closeness to Him. By intentionally giving God a place in our agenda, we align our plans with His will and ensure that our time is spent in ways that honour Him.

The Bible encourages us to begin our day by focusing on God: *"My voice You shall hear in the morning, O Lord; in the morning I will direct it to You, and I will look up"* (Psalm 5:3, NKJV). This verse highlights the importance of starting our day with prayer and seeking God's guidance. When we open our eyes each morning, let us remember to say good morning to God, acknowledging His presence and inviting Him into our day.

Our schedules often become packed with tasks and commitments, but setting aside dedicated time for prayer is essential. Mark 1:35 shows us Jesus's example: *"Very early in the morning, while it was still dark, Jesus got up, left the house and went off to a solitary place, where he prayed."* Jesus prioritized prayer by starting His day early and finding a quiet place to communicate with God. By following His example, we can ensure that prayer is a central part of our daily routine.

Proverbs 16:3 instructs, *"Commit to the Lord whatever you do, and he will establish your plans."* This verse emphasizes the importance of committing our plans and schedules to God. By giving Him a place in our agenda, we invite His guidance and blessing on our endeavours. Setting aside specific times for prayer and reflection ensures that we remain focused on God throughout the day.

According to Colossians 3:23, *"Whatever you do, work at it with all your heart, as working for the Lord, not for human masters."* This reminds us that our daily work should be done with a heart dedicated to God. Balancing our tasks with faith involves integrating our spiritual commitments with our professional and personal duties, ensuring that all aspects of our schedule honour Him.

James 1:5 encourages us to seek God's wisdom: *"If any of you lacks wisdom, you should ask God, who gives generously to all without finding fault, and it will be given to you."* When planning our schedules, we should ask God for wisdom to make decisions that reflect His will. This means consulting Him when setting priorities and making time for activities that support our spiritual growth and well-being.

Establishing a routine that includes time for prayer and Bible study helps us stay spiritually focused. Psalm 119:105 says, *"Your word is a lamp for my feet, a light on my path."* By incorporating God's Word into our daily routine, we gain direction and clarity for our schedule, ensuring that our activities align with His purposes.

By intentionally scheduling time for God, we show that He is our top priority. As we plan our day, let us remember to seek His presence, involve Him in our decisions, and dedicate time for prayer and reflection. This practice helps us stay centred on His will and ensures that our daily activities are aligned with our faith.

As I pray for God to be first in my schedule, I ask Him to guide my daily activities and help me maintain a balance between my responsibilities and spiritual commitments while remaining flexible to manage disruptions to my planning with grace. I will say in the morning, "This is the day that the Lord has made. Thanks for the gift of a new day. Help me to rejoice and be glad in it. May everything I do, think, and omit align to the values of your kingdom to which I belong."

Talking about giving God first place in my schedule doesn't mean that I won't fail many times. It's easier said than done, especially with a packed agenda, to be ready for God to shuffle our plans as needed to answer His call.

Recently, I felt a deep heaviness in my heart while reflecting on my former fitness instructor. Joe was a kind man who showed care for others in small, meaningful ways, like opening the gym door early on cold mornings so I wouldn't have to wait outside.

Though I hadn't seen him in months, I learned from a friend at the gym that he had fallen gravely ill and been diagnosed with cancer. When I texted Joe to ask how I could pray for him, his response was simple: "Just keep happy thoughts."

One day I found my friend was crying at the fitness club. She told me that she had visited Joe at the hospital and seen that his suffering was so severe that the staff were planning to administer a final shot three days later to allow him to pass peacefully.

When I heard about his deteriorating condition, I knew that I had to act. Yet instead of going immediately—understanding the urgency of the situation—I selfishly postponed it for the next day, which would be my birthday. I was thinking of it as a "gift" to myself. Looking back, I realize how wrong that was. I placed my own comfort and convenience over God's call to act in the here and now.

The following day, when I finally went to visit Joe at the hospital, ready to pray with him and share Jesus, the nurse informed me that he had passed the day before—just hours after I had learned of his condition. I was overcome with bitter regret and my tears flowing freely. I questioned whether I had missed a divine opportunity to introduce Joe to Jesus.

This stirred in me a compulsion to visit hospitals, even once a month, to pray for and with people and introduce them to the Lord as He leads. Many are suffering alone or may not know Him. It is our duty, as the church, to fulfill the Great Commission and carry His love to them.

In my grief, I found comfort in knowing that, although I failed to act promptly, God is never late. His plans are perfect and He surely reached out to Joe in ways I cannot fathom. As Jesus said in Luke 19:40, *"If they keep quiet, the stones will cry out."* I am reminded that God is sovereign and His love is relentless even when we falter.

The experience taught me a profound lesson: we must slow down, listen to God, and seize the moments He gives us to love others. Psalm 127:2 reminds us, *"It is vain for you to rise up early, to sit up late, to eat the bread of sorrows; for so He gives His beloved sleep"* (NKJV). I was too busy, like Martha, chasing time while God's invitation was to be with Joe in his final moments and sit at His feet, like Mary.

Inspired by this, I now feel led to commit to taking a sister in Christ out for fellowship at least once every other month, to accept a call for coffee, or to listen respectfully to a sister who needs to talk. It is so refreshing and fulfilling to take time to connect with others. It brings joy to my heart, and I know it pleases the Lord.

As God's children, let us not delay when He nudges our hearts. His call often comes in the form of simple opportunities—to pray, fellowship, and share His love. While we may falter, His plans never fail. May we live with open hands and open schedules, trusting Him to lead us in His perfect timing.

I encourage you to set aside dedicated time for God in your daily schedule—starting each day with Him, seeking His guidance throughout, and calling upon Him at night when you lay your head down to sleep. As you rest, trusting that He will watch over you, remember that while you sleep, He never does. As Psalm 121:3–4 says, *"He will not let your foot slip—he who watches over you will not slumber; indeed, he who watches over Israel will neither slumber nor sleep."*

We must be open to having our schedules shuffled according to God's plans, shifting our attitude from one of complaint to one of acceptance. It can be difficult when things don't go as we expect, but we can trust that God knows what's best. He sees the bigger picture and will redeem our time, for we never lose with Him. We may not always understand His timing, but we can rest assured that His watchful care will guide us through the day and night. Let us lean into this truth, knowing that God is always at work, even in the moments we don't see.

By doing so, we honour Him with our time and align our lives with His divine plan. Prioritizing God's kingdom in our daily schedules ensures that everything else falls into place according to His will. I have found it is one of the best way to redeem our time is to place the time He has given us back in the hand of the one who created time.

T is for troubles. In life, troubles are inevitable. Whether they come in the form of personal struggles, external pressures, or unexpected crises, how we respond to these difficulties reveals where we place our trust.

As believers, God calls us to run to Him first in our troubles, relying on His strength, wisdom, and comfort to guide us through. When troubles arise in my life, I run to the throne before I run to the phone. It's so easy to reach out to our best friend or spouse instead of our first love, God.

As I age, I more and more come to realize that troubles have ways of showing up without invitation even on the best days. If we don't have a safe place to run, we can live from frustration to frustration, which can be tough on our mental and physical health.

Recently, I had an almost perfect day. I woke up in a right spirit and had my quiet time with the Lord. But as I was driving, my baby girl, while eating a snack in the back seat, bit her tongue so bad that she was bleeding. Amidst her crying, I parked, got out, and went around to the passenger seat. In the process, I closed my finger in the car door. Now I was bleeding profusely too! The pain was so had that I thought I was going to pass out.

I managed to get to my daughter—but instead of me comforting her, she was the one comforting me.

"Oh Mommy, it hurts," she told me. "You are bleeding like me. Don't cry. I will pray for you. God will make you feel better."

Aww. This little angel made my day at that moment! She ran to God during this time of trouble, which gives me great relief.

Psalm 46:1 reassures us, *"God is our refuge and strength, a very present help in trouble"* (NKJV). God is always near, ready to help us when we face difficulties. Instead of turning to people, places, or things first, we should seek God's presence and guidance. He is our ultimate source of comfort and security, and He invites us to bring our troubles to Him.

In 1 Peter 5:7, we are encouraged, *"Cast all your anxiety on him because he cares for you."* God cares deeply about every aspect of our lives, including our worries and fears. When troubles arise, we should not carry the burden alone. Instead we are called to cast our anxieties on God, trusting that He will provide the strength and peace we need.

Philippians 4:6–7 offers practical advice for dealing with troubles:

> Do not be anxious about anything, but in every situation, by prayer and petition, with thanksgiving, present your requests to God. And the peace of God, which transcends all understanding, will guard your hearts and your minds in Christ Jesus.

When we bring our troubles to God in prayer, we open ourselves to His peace, which can calm our hearts and minds even in the midst of turmoil. This peace is a powerful reminder that God is in control. We are not alone in our struggles.

Our understanding is limited, and true wisdom comes from God. It's natural to seek advice from others when we face problems, but God desires to be the first one we turn to. And you know what? Life has taught me that it's important to ask God who we should turn to before we decide first. Have you ever experienced huge trouble and reached out to someone who wasn't available and nowhere to be found? Worse, maybe you found them and realized that they didn't care much about your troubles. I have.

It's important not to lean on your own understanding. Put your expectations on God to guide you. The right person just might call you at the right moment, confirming that God is answering your prayer.

By seeking Him first, we demonstrate our trust in His perfect plan and open ourselves to His direction.

The Bible is filled with examples of individuals who turned to God in their times of trouble. One powerful example is King David, who consistently sought God's guidance and help during his reign. In Psalm 34:4, David writes, *"I sought the Lord, and he answered me; he delivered me from all my fears."* His life was full of challenges, yet he continually relied on God's faithfulness and God delivered him from his troubles.

Another example is found in the story of Jehoshaphat, a king of Judah who had to face a vast army. Instead of panicking or seeking human help first, Jehoshaphat sought the Lord. In 2 Chronicles 20:12, he prayed, *"Our God, will you not judge them? For we have no power to face this vast army that is attacking us. We do not know what to do, but our eyes are on you."* God responded to Jehoshaphat's faith by delivering Judah from its enemies, demonstrating His power and faithfulness.

I love the story of King Hezekiah, who received a threatening letter from the Assyrian King Sennacherib. Hezekiah took the letter to the temple and spread it out before the Lord in prayer. This account is found in 2 Kings 19:14–15:

> Hezekiah received the letter from the messengers and read it. Then he went up to the temple of the Lord and spread it out before the Lord. And Hezekiah prayed to the Lord: "Lord, the God of Israel, enthroned between the cherubim, you alone are God over all the kingdoms of the earth. You have made heaven and earth."

Hezekiah didn't call his army or start strategizing about his plans to retaliate. Instead he brought the letter to God. This passage illustrates his faith and trust in God in the face of a grave threat.

How about you? Do you trust God enough to go to Him first when you're in trouble?

Isaiah 41:10 offers a powerful promise from God: *"So do not fear, for I am with you; do not be dismayed, for I am your God. I will strengthen you and help you; I will uphold you with my righteous right hand."* In times of trouble, God assures us that He is with us, providing strength and support. This promise gives us the confidence to face our challenges with faith, knowing that God will sustain us.

Romans 8:28 reminds us, *"And we know that in all things God works for the good of those who love him, who have been called according to his purpose."* Even in our darkest moments, God is working behind the scenes for our good. Trusting in His sovereignty allows us to find hope and purpose in our troubles, knowing that He can bring about good from even the most difficult circumstances. God invites us to cast our burdens on Him, trusting in His care and provision.

When troubles come, let us run to God first, placing our trust in Him before turning to any other source. By seeking Him in prayer, casting our burdens on Him, and finding strength in His promises, we can navigate life's challenges with confidence and peace.

> *When troubles come, let us run to God first, placing our trust in Him before turning to any other source.*

As I pray for God to be first in my troubles, I ask Him to guide me through every difficulty, to be my refuge and strength, and to help me trust in His perfect plan. I encourage you to make God your first resort in times of trouble, relying on His wisdom, comfort, and provision to carry you through.

If this resonates with you, I encourage you to use the acronym FIRST in your prayers as often as you pray. Ask God to be first in your finances, interests, relationships, schedules, and troubles.

2. Obedience in action, aligning our lives with God's commands. My second prayer essential is to obey Him wholeheartedly. Obedience matters to our heavenly Father more than anything else. Through our obedience, His blessings can flow. Because He is just, He cannot go against His own commands. He cannot bless disobedience.

The word obey has its roots in *obeir*, a French verb that ultimately derives from the Latin word *oboedire*, which means to "pay attention" and "listen to."[4] In the Bible, particularly in passages like Ephesians

---

[4] "Obey," *Online Etymology Dictionary*. Date of access: December 16, 2024 (https://www.etymonline.com/word/obey).

6:1–2, the word obey carries the connotation of submitting to authority, particularly to God's commands or those in positions of authority God has established, such as parents. The etymology of the word suggests that obedience involves not just outward compliance but also attentive listening and submission. In the biblical context, obedience is often linked with faith and trust in God, recognizing His sovereignty and wisdom in guiding one's life.

Therefore, to obey in the biblical sense implies not only following directives but doing so with a willing heart, acknowledging God's authority and seeking to align one's actions with His will. This obedience is seen as essential for a faithful and fruitful relationship with God and for experiencing His blessings and guidance in life.

We read the parable of the two sons in Matthew 21:28–32:

> "What do you think? There was a man who had two sons. He went to the first and said, 'Son, go and work today in the vineyard.'
>
> "'I will not,' he answered, but later he changed his mind and went.
>
> "Then the father went to the other son and said the same thing. He answered, 'I will, sir,' but he did not go.
>
> "Which of the two did what his father wanted?"
>
> "The first," they answered.
>
> Jesus said to them, "Truly I tell you, the tax collectors and the prostitutes are entering the kingdom of God ahead of you. For John came to you to show you the way of righteousness, and you did not believe him, but the tax collectors and the prostitutes did. And even after you saw this, you did not repent and believe him."

That's powerful, isn't it? We are not saved merely by saying, "Lord, Lord," or "Alleluia, Alleluia." Matthew 7:21–23 makes this clear:

> Not everyone who says to me, "Lord, Lord," will enter the kingdom of heaven, but only the one who does the will of my Father who is in heaven. Many will say to me on that day, "Lord, Lord, did we not prophesy in your name and in your name drive out demons and in your name perform many miracles?" Then I will tell them plainly, "I never knew you. Away from me, you evildoers!"

This passage, part of Jesus's sermon on the mount, emphasizes the importance of obeying God's will rather than merely professing faith with words. Jesus warns against superficial obedience, such as seen in those who merely call on His name without living according to God's commandments.

These passages in Matthew highlights the difference between outward religious actions and genuine obedience to God. They teach that true discipleship involves not just words or actions done for show, but a deep and sincere commitment to living according to God's will. This calls believers to examine their faith and ensure that it is rooted in genuine love and obedience to God, not just religious rituals or declarations.

You may have noticed that since you started reading this book, I haven't mentioned denominational groups. This is because I have come to realize the truth of what we read in James 1:27: *"Religion that God our Father accepts as pure and faultless is this: to look after orphans and widows in their distress and to keep oneself from being polluted by the world."*

My God, the heavenly Father I serve, didn't bring religion but relationship. We are not His children because we are Catholic, Protestant, or Baptist. We are His children because we look after the needy, such as orphans, widows, or those in distress, whether through a word of encouragement or in practical ways. This keeps us from being polluted by the world. In other words, we avoid being influenced or corrupted by the sinful patterns, values, and behaviours prevalent in society. The world, in this context, refers to anything that stands in opposition to God's ways—desires, pride, selfishness, materialism, and immorality.

One verse that explains the way of the world well is 1 John 2:15–17:

> Do not love the world or anything in the world. If anyone loves the world, love for the Father is not in them. For everything in the world—the lust of the flesh, the lust of the eyes, and the pride of life—comes not from the Father but from the world. The world and its desires pass away, but whoever does the will of God lives forever.

This passage highlights three truths about worldly pollution:

1. The lust of the flesh. This refers to sinful desires that seek to satisfy the physical body, often in ways that are contrary to God's commandments.
2. The lust of the eyes. This speaks to the covetousness and greed that arise from focusing on material wealth and possessions.
3. The pride of life. This is the arrogance and self-sufficiency that come from relying on one's own accomplishments, status, or power rather than humbly submitting to God.

To keep oneself from being polluted by the world, a believer must consciously reject these worldly temptations and instead pursue a life that is pleasing to God—one that is characterized by humility, purity, self-control, and a deep love for others. This involves daily surrender to God, renewing one's mind with His Word and allowing the Holy Spirit to guide one's actions and decisions.

The epistle of James is a practical letter emphasizing the importance of living out one's faith through actions. James contrasts superficial religious practices with the kind of religion that truly pleases God, one that involves compassionate care for the most vulnerable in society and personal moral integrity.

Together, these passages of scripture remind us that true faith is reflected in actions that align with God's will—caring for others, living righteously, and sincerely following God's commandments.

After obeying the first commandment to love God first and foremost, my duty is to obey Him. I use OBEY as an acrostic.

O is for obeying Him through actions, not merely words. We read in 1 Samuel 15:22, *"Does the Lord delight in burnt offerings and sacrifices as much as in obeying the Lord? To obey is better than sacrifice, and to heed is better than the fat of rams."*

The best sacrifice we can give to God, and gift to ourselves, is to obey His commands. This is the best gift our heavenly Father expects from us. He will not force us to obey because of the free will He gives us. He shows us the consequences of obedience and disobedience and asks us to use our free will to obey simply because it's for our own good. It's a sign of the love we have for God, as it is written in John 14:23–24:

> Jesus replied, "Anyone who loves me will obey my teaching. My Father will love them, and we will come to them and make our home with them. Anyone who does not love me will not obey my teaching. These words you hear are not my own; they belong to the Father who sent me."

Powerful, isn't it? Our love for God avails nothing if we don't obey Him.

Do you remember my first prayer essential? I asked God to help me to love Him with all my heart, mind, and soul. And obeying His commands, when I put Him first in my life, is God's love language. Moreover, God's Word clearly tells us, *"Do not merely listen to the word, and so deceive yourselves. Do what it says"* (James 1:22).

I have found lately that it's hard for people to obey. But you know what? We all obey the authorities. When we go shopping, we cannot refuse to pay the taxes. If we work on a certain schedule, we cannot decide to change that schedule whenever we want. It's hard to obey God. Instead we make excuses, as if obeying God is for His own good. But it's for our own good. His compassionate heart doesn't impose obedience on us. He shows us the way and lets us use our free will.

As for me, I choose to obey because I know it's for my good. And to be able to do so, I need God's help to do what the Word says at all times, not just when I feel like it. I don't pick and choose what I like about His Word, like dishes at a buffet.

B is for binding ourselves to God's commands. By choosing to obey God, I consider myself bound to His commands. The concept of being bound implies a deep commitment, a connection that isn't easily broken.

In the Bible, the idea of being bound has its roots in the language of covenants and servitude, often symbolizing a binding agreement or commitment to God.

In the Old Testament, covenants between God and His people often involved binding agreements. For example, God's covenant with Abraham was a binding promise (Genesis 17). To be bound to God's commands can be seen to mean that we must live under the terms of such a covenant; obedience is a key element of the relationship.

To be honest, I've always considered myself a free spirit, much like a wild bird. I haven't wanted to be bound to anything. I've wanted to be free to do whatever I want, however I want, without restriction.

My relationship with God has been a roller-coaster. I have been a prodigal daughter for a long time, repeatedly finding myself back in the same situations, learning the same lessons over and over again, because I haven't wanted to obey. I thought I knew better, that I knew it all.

Have you experienced that? Even if it is only in certain areas of your life?

When God tells us that we have free will, I have taken that literally, interpreting it to mean that I could go my own way. And I did. But let me confess here that it's not worth it. God's commandments have been given to us for our good. Consider parents who love their children so much that they warn them not to touch a fire. If the children believe the fire is too beautiful to resist, they will pay the consequences. It will hurt the parents' hearts, but the children will be the ones to suffer most.

I have been burnt a lot and suffered great harm because of my disobedience.

This is why I encourage you to know God's commands and abide by them. I'm confident that it's the best way, because I haven't always been malleable clay in the hands of the Potter. But He has allowed my disobedience to break me many times so I could reach the stage I'm at today—a place of wholehearted obedience, surrendering all to Him. He has not given up on me. He's pursued me to save me from dying in my sins.

He won't give up on you either. For God to work in your life and make a masterpiece of you, He has to break you, starting over with you many times and shaping you to make you more like Him. It will only happen when you decide to be bound to God's commands.

In Ephesians 6:6, we read that we are to obey Him *"not by way of eye-service, as people-pleasers, but as bondservants of Christ, doing the will of God from the heart"* (ESV). The term bondservants in this verse refers to individuals who willingly serve Christ out of devotion and commitment. It originates from the Greek word *doulos*, which is used in the New Testament, particularly by Paul, to describe a willing servant of Christ (Romans 1:1, Philippians 1:1). It translates to slave, or servant.

However, in the biblical context, being a bondservant of Christ implies a voluntary and devoted commitment rather than forced servitude. This term reflects a voluntary, committed service, indicating a person who is bound to serve another by choice. Similarly, being bound to God's commands reflects a willing submission and commitment to follow His will.

The term *doulos* carries connotations of absolute devotion, loyalty, and obedience to the master. In this verse, Paul instructs believers to serve Christ wholeheartedly, not merely to please others or fulfill outward appearances. Instead their service should be genuine and sincere, driven by their devotion to Christ and a desire to do His will.

By emphasizing that believers are bondservants of Christ, Paul highlights the intimate and profound relationship between the believer and their Savior. It signifies a willing surrender of one's life, desires, and ambitions to Christ, acknowledging Him as the ultimate authority and master. As bondservants of Christ, believers are called to serve Him with integrity, sincerity, and genuine devotion, seeking to fulfill His will from the depths of their hearts.

By choosing to obey God, I am bound to Him. We cannot obey God in our own power and strength; we need God's help to make it through. Mentors, pastors, and Christian friends might give up on us after our many failures. They may become discouraged, run out of patience, or think we're not genuine and will never change. But God, who knows us better than we know ourselves and has placed more in us than we can imagine, will never give up on us. He sees us and has been at work in us from the beginning of time.

I am His servant. I am bound to His commands. I declare, following Psalm 119:30–32,

> I have chosen the way of faithfulness; I have set my heart on your laws. I hold fast to your statutes, Lord; do not let me be put to shame. I run in the path of your commands, for you have broadened my understanding.

When I say that I'm bound to God's commands, I am expressing a voluntary and deep commitment to live according to God's will. It means that I have chosen to tie myself to God's teachings, allowing them to guide and shape my life. This commitment isn't superficial or temporary. It's a lifelong journey of obedience, akin to being in a covenant relationship with God.

It's also a transformation process. Being bound to God allows Him to work in my life, moulding and refining me just as a potter shapes clay. The breaking and reshaping I describe signify the ongoing process of spiritual growth and maturity. I need God's help to obey His commands—and you, too, will need His help to surrender to His commands.

Why not ask Him in prayer?

E is for embracing every opportunity to obey. The law in our country says, "Do not kill." That's not just a public prohibition, with the caveat that we can kill in private. Either way we would be prosecuted and pay the consequences.

We cannot decide one year to declare and pay our taxes and then fail to do so the next because we don't feel like it. We have to do it every year.

In the same way, obedience to God should not be conditional or selective. As we read in Deuteronomy 10:12–13,

> And now, Israel, what does the Lord your God ask of you but to fear the Lord your God, to walk in obedience to him, to love him, to serve the Lord your God with all your heart and with all your soul, and to observe the Lord's commands and decrees that I am giving you today for your own good?

We shouldn't embrace obedience only when it's convenient. Our obedience to God must be consistent, whether we're at church, home, or work. We should be the same person in public and in private. The proof of a virtuous person is often revealed in how they behave when no one is watching. It's easy to wear masks, please people, and present ourselves in a way that's different from who we really are, but God wants His children to be genuine.

The psalmist expressed this well in Psalm 119:44: *"I will always obey your law, for ever and ever."*

Embracing every opportunity to obey means being committed to following God's commands in all circumstances, at all times, and in every place. As Philippians 2:12 says, *"Therefore, my dear friends, as you have always obeyed—not only in my presence, but now much more in my absence—continue to work out your salvation with fear and trembling…"*

Obedience means living consistently with integrity, allowing God's commands to shape who we are and how we act in every aspect of our lives. It's not something we can do by our own will and strength; we need God's help.

I needed God's help to choose not to follow my desires and will but to follow His instead. That's why I asked Him to help me embrace every opportunity that comes my way to obey His will, not mine. How about you?

Y is for yielding our will to God. We have already defined yielding in the first portion of the breath prayer section, but let's dive a little deeper.

I want to be sincere: human beings don't naturally like to yield control. Even babies, who obviously don't yet know how to speak or walk, will stubbornly hold onto their toys, unwilling to let go. We are the same as adults.

But yielding is necessary in order for God's will to take over in our lives. Even Jesus had to yield His will to the will of the Father, as He declared in Luke 22:42: *"Father, if you are willing, take this cup from me; yet not my will, but yours be done."* Jesus is our model of obedience. He was obedient to the point of death. He taught us that obedience to God's commands is never easy. But when we yield to God's will, the impossible becomes possible and the hard becomes easy.

Throughout the Bible, we see examples of individuals who yielded to God's will, often at great personal cost but with profound outcomes. Abraham yielded to God's will by agreeing to sacrifice his son Isaac. This demonstrated his trust in God's promise, even when it seemed impossible.

When it came to trusting God's promise of a son, however, Abraham did not fully yield—not at first. He followed his wife Sarah's suggestion to have a child with Hagar, thinking he could lend God a hand since he and Sarah were getting old.

> But God does not need our help; He needs our obedience.

But God does not need our help; He needs our obedience.

It can be easier to yield in some areas and not in others, as we all have our strengths and weaknesses. Know your weaknesses and surrender them to God because the enemy of your soul will use these weaknesses to tempt you and cause you to fall. Always remember James 1:14–15, which says, *"But each one is tempted when he is drawn away by his own desires and enticed. Then, when desire has conceived, it gives birth to sin; and sin, when it is full-grown, brings forth death"* (NKJV). For example, if lust is your weakness, the enemy will use it. Beware, my friends.

The Bible contains many other examples of people yielding to God, such as the apostle Paul. After his dramatic conversion on the road to Damascus (Acts 9), Paul yielded his life to God's will, dedicating himself to spreading the gospel.

This is why it is critical to meditate on God's Word day and night and let it light our path (Psalm 119:105). We must read the Bible in order for us to gain the strength to yield our lives to Him. The Word of God instructs us,

> This Book of the Law shall not depart from your mouth, but you shall meditate in it day and night, that you may observe to do according to all that is written in it. For then you will make your way prosperous, and then you will have good success. (Joshua 1:8, NKJV)

God's Word reveals His will and teaches us how to align our thoughts, actions, and desires with His purposes. As we immerse ourselves in Scripture, we gain the wisdom and strength to obey God and yield to His will, trusting that He knows what's best for us.

As we pray for God's help to obey Him, let us commit to applying the OBEY acrostic, allowing it to guide our hearts and actions each day.

3. Loving my neighbour as myself, embracing the second greatest commandment. My third prayer essential is about asking God to help me obey the second commandment, which is to love my neighbour as myself.

In Matthew 22:37–39, Jesus says,

> "Love the Lord your God with all your heart and with all your soul and with all your mind." This is the first and greatest commandment. And the second is like it: "Love your neighbor as yourself."

Jesus emphasizes that the entire law is fulfilled in these two commandments—loving God and loving others. The second commandment, "Love your neighbour as yourself," is significant because it extends the love we have for God into our relationships with others. By loving others, we demonstrate God's love in a tangible way, fulfilling His law.

I don't know about you, but to be honest this verse has been extremely difficult for me. On many levels, I have struggled with the concept of love. What is love? I wasn't raised in a Christian family and my father had ten kids with seven women, even though polygamy wasn't legal. Culturally, men often showed how "irresistible" they were by collecting women. It was all about proving how macho they were.

I was mostly raised by my mom, and I saw how heartbroken she was. My dad was the first and only man she ever knew. When my dad wasn't around, I walked on eggshells trying to please her, to give her something she didn't have.

So the concept of love, for me, became transactional: you have to do something to be loved. Otherwise you won't be loved; you'll be rejected. And if you're not enough, like my mom wasn't enough, you'll be rejected and suffer. I wanted to be enough—that is, until life taught me that our best will never be good enough for those who don't love us.

But those who love you will love you through your worst.

When I started to relearn what love truly is from my heavenly Father, I found the answer in 1 Corinthians 13:4–7:

> Love is patient, love is kind. It does not envy, it does not boast, it is not proud. It does not dishonor others, it is not self-seeking, it is not easily angered, it keeps no record of wrongs. Love does not delight in evil but rejoices with the truth. It always protects, always trusts, always hopes, always perseveres.

This is what the second commandment from my heavenly Father asks me to do: be patient, kind, not envious or boastful, not arrogant or rude, not irritable or resentful, not rejoicing at wrongdoing, but rejoicing with the truth. I'm called to bear, believe, hope, and endure all things.

My first response was simple: "Really? Be my guest." I didn't want to do all of that. It seemed like a lot. I didn't think I could do it. I didn't feel I even possessed those qualities myself. And we can only give what we have, right?

In 1 John 4:20–21, I read,

> Whoever claims to love God yet hates a brother or sister is a liar. For whoever does not love their brother and sister, whom they have seen, cannot love God,

whom they have not seen. And he has given us this command: Anyone who loves God must also love their brother and sister.

Oh my goodness! According to this, I couldn't say I loved God if I didn't love my own brother and sister? That was too much!

It would be so much easier to love a God who was lovely, compassionate, just, and full of positive attributes. But I couldn't always say that about my neighbours.

This passage made it clear that one's love for God is inseparable from one's love for others. So if we cannot love those around us—people we see and interact with—how can we truly love God, whom we have not seen? Genuine love for God naturally flows into love for others, and failing to love others indicates a lack of genuine love for God.

James 2:8 says, *"If you really keep the royal law found in Scripture, 'Love your neighbor as yourself,' you are doing right."* This reminded me of one of my role models, Joyce Meyer, as well as many others who insist that love is a choice, not a feeling.

I don't have to feel like I love you, but I can choose to be patient and kind, not rude or arrogant or envious, and in doing so I will love you. To choose to love my neighbour, I have to put my feelings aside and yield them to God.

James refers to the command to love our neighbour as the "royal law," emphasizing its supreme importance in the Christian life. This command is foundational because it encapsulates the essence of the entire law—living in a way that reflects God's love and righteousness.

I also found blessings in loving people in 1 Peter 4:8: *"Above all, love each other deeply, because love covers over a multitude of sins."* This highlights the power of love in relationships. When we love deeply, we are willing to overlook the faults and failures of others, just as God does with us. Love leads to forgiveness and reconciliation, maintaining unity and peace in the community of believers.

This is how I came to decide that love is a choice. I've embraced Paul's command in Romans 13:8–10, which states,

> Let no debt remain outstanding, except the continuing debt to love one another, for whoever loves others has fulfilled the law. The commandments, "You shall not commit adultery," "You shall not murder," "You shall not steal," "You shall not covet," and whatever other command there may be, are summed up in this one command: "Love your neighbor as yourself." Love does no harm to a neighbor. Therefore love is the fulfillment of the law.

Whoever fulfills these two commandments has fulfilled the law. So I could not escape this part. And I needed God's help to do so.

But then I started wrestling with the key question: who is my neighbour? This concept challenged me. The verse could have told me to love my family, my children, or my spouse, but instead it told me to love my neighbour. Who is that?

The answer comes in Luke 10:25–37 when a lawyer asked Jesus that exact question. In response, Jesus told the parable of a man who was attacked by robbers and left for dead on the side of the road. A priest and a Levite, both religious figures, passed by without helping him. However, a Samaritan, a group despised by Jews at the time, stopped to help. He tended to the man's wounds, took him to an inn, and paid for his care.

After telling the parable, Jesus and the lawyer had a dialogue:

> "Which of these three do you think was a neighbor to the man who fell into the hands of robbers?"
> The expert in the law replied, "The one who had mercy on him."
> Jesus told him, "Go and do likewise." (Luke 10:36–37)

Jesus expands the definition of neighbour beyond one's immediate community. It doesn't just apply to people with whom we share similar beliefs or backgrounds. He teaches that our neighbour is anyone in need, regardless of their nationality, religion, or social status.

Really?

So my neighbour is the person on the bus who steps on my toes, the friend who uses and betrays me, and the coworkers who gossip about me. It's everyone. The command to love our neighbour as ourselves calls us to show compassion, kindness, and mercy to all people, just as the Samaritan did.

This parable emphasizes the reality that neighbourly love is about actions, not just feelings. We are required to help others in practical ways, even if it involves personal sacrifice.

Not only do I have to love as the Bible defines love, but I also have to love everyone. And the most challenging part is that I must love them as I love myself. It's not easy. And how do we respond to the people who require extra grace, the ones who hurt us? We need to respond to them in love.

In 1 John 4:7, we are commanded, *"Beloved, let us love one another, for love is of God; and everyone who loves is born of God and knows God"* (NKJV). This highlights our ability to love others, which stems from our relationship with God. By placing God at the centre of our relationships, we reflect His love and character to those around us.

Jesus also emphasizes the importance of loving others:

> A new commandment I give to you, that you love one another; as I have loved you, that you also love one another. By this all will know that you are My disciples, if you have love for one another. (John 13:34–35, NKJV)

Love is the hallmark of a true Christian and should define our interactions with others. Therefore, in the family of God, it is a must to love one another.

> So he answered and said, "'You shall love the Lord your God with all your heart, with all your soul, with all your strength, and with all your mind,' and 'your neighbor as yourself.'" (Luke 10:27, NKJV)

This verse, which speaks of loving one's neighbour as oneself, teaches us that loving God wholly also impacts how we love others. It reminds us that our love for God is not just an inward feeling; it should extend outwardly to those around us.

Reflecting on my upbringing and the pain I endured during childhood, I realize how challenging it can be to love others.

As a child, I was abused by an uncle who was entrusted to watch over me so my mom could go to work. Instead he would wait for her to leave the house, then put alcohol in my bottle to make me sleep all day. This allowed him to leave me alone in the house while he went about his own business. This was followed by other assaults and more verbal abuse, all of which left me deeply bruised inside.

But God's love reached me even at a young age.

At three years old, I was excited to start school and finally be with other children. However, my joy was short-lived when I experienced bullying. The other kids bullied me and ate my lunch, leaving me in tears by the end of each day. In the country I grew up in, it was considered normal for kids to fight. Because it was seen as a way to build character, no adults intervened.

One person did stand by me. Guerlyne became my first friend. The next day, when I was physically beaten and had my lunchbox taken again, she fought back for me, retrieved my lunchbox, and sat with me to eat. She became my buddy and we've never been apart since then, more than forty years later. I felt I had nothing to give her in return, yet she asked for nothing. She was simply there for me.

God has challenged me to love, no matter the pain or rejection I've faced. He has shown His love for me not only by loving me first but by sending loving people into my life in incredible ways.

While I've encountered some wonderful people who have loved me deeply, I've also faced those who lied to me, rejected me, and caused me pain.

When I became a Fulbright scholar, I moved with my daughters to Oakland, California for a time to pursue my MBA. I met some of my greatest supporters there, Warrine, Bill, Nancy, and Bryce. Although not related by blood, they embraced me and my daughters. They loved us unconditionally, without question. They weren't pushy and they didn't ask for anything in return. They were simply there for us, offering support and showing what true unconditional love looks like.

Later I met David Katz, who along with his wife Taylor demonstrated what it means to love unconditionally. Their love in action has been a guiding light in my life.

In stark contrast, when I was pregnant with one of my daughters and had to travel, a Christian couple I had known for decades initially invited me to stay in their home for two weeks. However, just three days later, they asked me to leave after I shared something personal about my life with them. They decided I wasn't "worthy" to stay in their home.

This experience stood in contrast to the example Jesus set during His ministry. He chose to spend time with sinners, tax collectors, and those marginalized by society. In Matthew 9, He was criticized for eating with sinners, but He responded by saying, *"It is not the healthy who need a doctor, but the sick... For I have not come to call the righteous, but sinners"* (Matthew 9:12–13).

Similarly, in Luke 19:1–10, Jesus dined with Zacchaeus, a tax collector, bringing light and transformation to his life.

These stories remind us that the best way to show the light of Christ is by stepping into the darkness, not by pushing it away. True Christian love and hospitality mean embracing others with compassion and grace, regardless of their circumstances, just as Jesus did.

For instance, I love my children and have chosen to always be there for them, no matter what. I don't request anything in return. I want them to naturally love me back, but I still choose to love them if they don't. This is what my perfect heavenly Father does with me.

Therefore, I have to aim to obey the second commandment to love my neighbour as myself, however hard it is.

When others turned against me and walked away at the first sign of difficulty, I learned to discern the difference and hold on to the love I knew to be true. The greatest love of my life comes from the one who gave it all for me, who loves me so much that *"He gave His only begotten Son, that whoever believes in Him should not perish but have everlasting life"* (John 3:16, NKJV).

It's hard to love people who hurt, abuse, or harm us. My natural tendency is to avoid them as much as possible. Reflecting on this, I came up with the term "amorkaemia," combining the Spanish word *amor* (love) with *kaemia* (from leukaemia). I suffer from amorkaemia. Just as someone with leukaemia needs regular blood transfusions to survive, I recognize that my natural blood doesn't allow me to love the unlovable. For that to happen, I need a regular transfusion of God's divine love.

I receive this transfusion through daily prayer, when I ask God to fill me with His love so I can learn to genuinely love others without expecting anything in return. This process isn't easy, but it is transformative. Despite the hurts and challenges I face, I can choose to love—not because I feel it, but because I am committed to reflecting God's love.

Loving in this way isn't about emotions; it's a deliberate choice to act with a kind and loving attitude, even when it's difficult.

How about you? Have you ever asked God for His love to flow through you when your own love feels inadequate?

4. Pursuing holiness, a Call to be set apart. We often hear about holiness, but what does the word mean? According to biblical etymology, it's translated from the Hebrew word *qadosh* and the Greek word *hagios*, both of which mean "set apart" or "sacred." Holiness signifies being set apart for God's purposes, embodying purity and moral integrity.

From the Old Testament to the New, God's command is clear: we are called to be holy because He is holy. In Leviticus 20:26, we read:

> You are to be holy to me because I, the Lord, am holy, and I have set you apart from the nations to be my own. (Leviticus 20:26)

> But just as he who called you is holy, so be holy in all you do; 16 for it is written: "Be holy, because I am holy." (1 Peter 1:15–16)

> Make every effort to live in peace with everyone and to be holy; without holiness no one will see the Lord. (Hebrews 12:14)

I want to see God. I don't know about you, but we all long to see the one we love.

Those who have met people online—friends, lovers, relatives, or even stranger—will agree that as the relationship deepens and strengthens, we long to see them person face to face. When we are physically separated from our loved ones, we long to see them. We miss them.

Yes, I want to see God—and without holiness, I won't see Him. Therefore I long to seek holiness so I can see Him.

God's call to holiness is not merely a suggestion but a divine mandate—an obligation. It isn't a buffet where you can take what you like and leave the rest.

So what is holiness? The world might call it honesty or integrity, which are great words, but for us believers the word is *holiness—and it* means being set apart for God. We are called to a holy life, one that reflects God's own nature. This calling isn't based on our merit but on His grace and purpose, as mentioned in 2 Timothy 1:9:

> He has saved us and called us to a holy life—not because of anything we have done but because of his own purpose and grace. This grace was given us in Christ Jesus before the beginning of time…

Holiness involves an ongoing process of purification as we strive to become more like Jesus in purity and character. It's not an abstract concept but something we live out daily. It involves offering ourselves to God and embodying His righteousness and holiness. If the Lord has given us the grace to be holy, it means we have to play our part, which is to seek, embrace, and accept that grace without doubt.

While I pray for God to help me walk a holy life, I need to know what this implies. How can I reach the standard of holiness? Romans 12:1–2 gives me the answer:

> I appeal to you therefore, brothers, by the mercies of God, to present your bodies as a living sacrifice, holy and acceptable to God, which is your spiritual worship.

> Do not be conformed to this world, but be transformed by the renewal of your mind, that by testing you may discern what is the will of God, what is good and acceptable and perfect. (ESV)

I needed time, teaching, and mentoring to unpack these concepts. I want to share with you what the Holy Spirit, who is my greatest teacher, has revealed to me. It is very important that we pray with knowledge of what we are praying about. Prayer is meditating.

> *It is very important that we pray with knowledge of what we are praying about. Prayer is meditating.*

Presenting my body as a living sacrifice to God in the pursuit of holiness implies taking care of *me*—all of me. And who is Sephora? Who are you? We are spirits, living in bodies, possessing souls. Just as the Lord God I have chosen to surrender my life to is one God in three persons—the Father, the Son, and the Holy Spirit—we, being created in His image, are also tripartite beings. Romans 8:16 confirms this: *"The Spirit himself testifies with our spirit that we are God's children."* Therefore, I need to take care of all three parts.

Starting with my physical health, this means taking care of my body through proper nutrition, exercise, and rest. As 1 Corinthians 6:19–20 states,

> Do you not know that your bodies are temples of the Holy Spirit, who is in you, whom you have received from God? You are not your own; you were bought at a price. Therefore honor God with your bodies.

I honour God when I avoid the abuse of drugs, alcohol, or anything that can defile this temple where the Spirit of God dwells.

Taking care of our bodies as Christian believers goes beyond physical health, though. It involves abstaining from sexual immorality and maintaining purity and holiness in every aspect.

In 1 Thessalonians 4:3–4, we are reminded: *"It is God's will that you should be sanctified: that you should avoid sexual immorality; that each of you should learn to control your own body in a way that is holy and honorable..."* Sanctification, being set apart for God's purposes, requires us to exercise self-control and live in a manner that is pleasing to Him. Sexual immorality, which includes any sexual activity outside the bounds of a biblically defined relationship, is not only a sin against our bodies but also against God, who created us to live in purity and honour.

Maintaining purity in our relationships reflects our commitment to God's standards and our respect for others. It involves more than just avoiding sinful actions; it requires us to cultivate a heart and mind that are aligned with God's will. This means guarding our thoughts, speech, and action and seeking to build relationships that are rooted in mutual respect, love, and godliness.

As believers, we are called to be different from the world around us, which often promotes and normalizes behaviours that are contrary to God's design. By abstaining from sexual immorality and pursuing purity, we demonstrate our dedication to living according to God's Word. This not only protects us from the physical, emotional, and spiritual consequences of sin but also allows us to experience the fullness of life that God intends for us.

Seeking holiness in my body also implies using my physical strength and abilities to serve others, as I read in Galatians 5:13: *"You, my brothers and sisters, were called to be free. But do not use your freedom to indulge the flesh; rather, serve one another humbly in love."*

Therefore, the practical way to love my neighbour as myself is to serve them in loving ways. It is not a feeling or an emotion, but a choice to serve.

Ultimately, taking care of our bodies and maintaining purity is an act of worship. It's our response to the love and grace God has shown us, and it is a testimony to the world of the transforming power of the gospel in our lives.

Offering my body as a living sacrifice also means taking care of my spirit. Since my soul, spirit, and body are one, I cannot disregard any part of them. Engaging in spiritual practices such as prayer, meditation, fasting, and worship should be my aim. Romans 12:12 invites me to *"be joyful in hope, patient in affliction, faithful in prayer."* Seeking holiness means being faithful in conversing with God, communicating with Him, and allowing Him to connect with me in many different ways. As Job 33:14 states: *"God speaks in different ways, and we don't always recognize his voice"* (CEV).

Seeking holiness also requires keeping my mind and thoughts holy. Who can claim they've never had a sinful thought? We might call these thoughts silly, unholy, or something else, but it's easy to pretend an outward attitude while our minds and hearts harbour negative, hurtful thoughts. Holiness reaches even there, and I am called to guard my heart and mind, as Philippians 4:8 advises: *"Finally, brothers and sisters, whatever is true, whatever is noble, whatever is right, whatever is pure, whatever is lovely, whatever is admirable—if anything is excellent or praiseworthy—think about such things."* This encourages me to avoid harmful media, conversations, environments that lead to sin, and influences that corrupt my thoughts and behaviours.

I remember reading that the eyes are the mirrors of the soul. What we watch eventually shapes our beliefs, imprints on our hearts, and influences how we show up. So what do you watch? Which type of movie? Television series? Video games?

I am called to seek holiness even in the secret places, where nobody else sees, because God sees, and He asks me to be holy as He is holy. As 1 Peter 1:15–16 states, *"But just as he who called you is holy, so be holy in all you do; for it is written: 'Be holy, because I am holy.'"* Since I believe I have been created in the image of my Lord and Savior, and as a daughter I have been called to be like my Father, I pray over my life: *"May God himself, the God of peace, sanctify you through and through. May your whole spirit, soul and body be kept blameless at the coming of our Lord Jesus Christ"* (1 Thessalonians 5:23).

My aim should be seeking holiness in everything I do. I do this not to please people or for others to see, but to please my Lord and Savior, as Colossians 3:23–24 instructs:

> Whatever you do, work at it with all your heart, as working for the Lord, not for human masters, since you know that you will receive an inheritance from the Lord as a reward. It is the Lord Christ you are serving.

What I truly appreciate about the Bible, which I have chosen to believe as the Word of God, is that it not only teaches me what to do but also what not to do. There's no room for guessing or missing the mark unless I choose not to see—because there is no worse blindness than refusing to see.

Romans 12:2 urges us, *"Do not conform to the pattern of this world, but be transformed by the renewing of your mind."* So let's explore some practical examples of the pattern of this world which believers are called to avoid, along with the corresponding biblical principles that encourage transformation.

The world relentlessly pursues wealth and possessions as primary sources of happiness and identity. However, the Word of God instructs us to *"seek first the kingdom of God and His righteousness"* (Matthew 6:33, NKJV) and to store up treasures in heaven (Matthew 6:19–21), which reflects the way of the kingdom. Prioritizing personal success and self-recognition above all else, often at the expense of others, is a common worldly pattern.

Yet believers are taught in Philippians 2:3–4 to embrace humility and serve others, considering their interests above their own.

The pursuit of financial gain at any cost, including exploiting others and engaging in dishonest practices, is another worldly trend. In contrast, Proverbs 11:1 and Acts 20:35 compel us to conduct business with integrity and generosity. The world often holds that truth and morality are subjective, varying based on personal or cultural preferences. Yet as believers we are called to adhere to God's unchanging truth and moral standards as revealed in Scripture (John 14:6, 2 Timothy 3:16–17).

Engaging in and normalizing behaviours such as premarital sex, adultery, and pornography is a pattern of this world. The Bible, however, commands us to honour God with our bodies and uphold sexual purity within marriage (1 Corinthians 6:18–20, Hebrews 13:4).

The world often justifies holding grudges and seeking revenge, but God calls us to forgive others as He has forgiven us and to pursue reconciliation (Ephesians 4:31–32, Matthew 6:14–15).

Additionally, while society pressures us to conform, even when it contradicts biblical values, we are urged to stand firm in our faith and be a light in the world (Romans 12:2, Matthew 5:14–16). Succumbing to feelings of despair and fear in life's challenges is common in the world.

This reminds me of life in the country where I grew up. Kidnapping was rampant and I was afraid for my life and the lives of my family. I had many nightmares. Then I started receiving death threats over the phone. When sharing my concerns with others, they encouraged me to hire bodyguards and private security. I had to trust in God for safety. Yet the Bible teaches us to trust in God's sovereignty and find hope and peace in Him (Jeremiah 29:11, Philippians 4:6–7). By recognizing and avoiding these patterns, believers can renew their minds and align their lives more closely with God's will and purpose.

Now that we have an idea of what the pattern of this world is, we need to develop practices for renewing the mind. We can be transformed by the renewing of our minds when we immerse ourselves in Scripture, studying and meditating on God's Word. Regularly reading and reflecting on the Bible helps us understand God's will and principles for living. Setting aside daily time for Bible study and memorization of key verses allows His truth to shape our thoughts and actions.

It is essential to engage in prayer and worship, as well as develop a consistent prayer life. Philippians 4:6 encourages us: *"Do not be anxious about anything, but in every situation, by prayer and petition, with thanksgiving, present your requests to God."* Incorporating times of prayer throughout the day and participating in corporate worship are vital if you want to experience both communal and personal renewal.

Embracing the mind of Christ means aligning our thoughts, attitudes, and behaviours with those of Jesus, focusing on humility, love, and service. Philippians 2:5 commands, *"Let this mind be in you which was also in Christ Jesus"* (NKJV). Practicing selflessness and compassion in our interactions allows us to serve others and reflect Christ's character in all aspects of life.

By implementing these practices, we can experience transformation through the renewing of our minds, aligning our lives more closely with God's will and purpose.

Hebrews 12:14 says, *"Make every effort to live in peace with everyone and to be holy; without holiness no one will see the Lord."* What does it mean not to see God? In the context of Hebrews 12:14, seeing the Lord can be understood both in a spiritual sense (experiencing God's presence and favour) and eschatologically (seeing God in the afterlife). Holiness is a requisite for this close relationship with God.

While holiness is a work of God's grace, it also requires human effort and cooperation with the Holy Spirit to grow in sanctification.

In summary, living a holy life involves a wholehearted commitment to God's ways, striving to reflect His character and maintaining purity in every aspect of life. Without this dedication to holiness, we will be hindered from experiencing a deep and intimate relationship with God that allows us to truly see Him, both now and in eternity.

5. Humility in grace, remembering the source of all blessings. I ask my Lord and Savior to keep me humble at all times. Given my background, culture, and upbringing, it was important for people to affirm themselves, to boast about what they knew and who they knew.

While self-confidence isn't inherently wrong, we fall short when we start to believe we are in control of everything. I've fallen short many times by relying on my own strength, which is why I need to humble myself before my Lord and Savior so He can lift me up. He promises in James 4:10, *"Humble yourselves before the Lord, and he will lift you up."*

The word humility comes from the Latin *humilitas*, a noun related to *humus*, referring either to the ground or earth. This etymology reminds us that humility is about recognizing our groundedness, connection to the earth, and dependence on God. In Greek, the word for humility is *tapeinophrosyne*, which translates to "lowliness of mind," a deep sense of one's own smallness and dependence on God's greatness.

Moses is described as having been *"more humble than anyone else on the face of the earth"* (Numbers 12:3). Despite leading Israel out of Egypt and receiving the Ten Commandments, Moses constantly depended on God and interceded for his people, putting their needs above his own.

Philippians 2:5–8 encourages us to have the same mindset as Christ:

> In your relationships with one another, have the same mindset as Christ Jesus: who, being in very nature God, did not consider equality with God something to be used to his own advantage; rather, he made himself nothing by taking the very nature of a servant, being made in human likeness. And being found in appearance as a man, he humbled himself by becoming obedient to death—even death on a cross!

Humility is foundational for those who follow Christ. Jesus Himself, the Son of God, exemplified ultimate humility by coming down from heaven, taking on human form, and sacrificing His life on the cross.

King David showed humility throughout his life, especially in his willingness to repent when confronted with his sins. In Psalm 51:17, David prays, *"My sacrifice, O God, is a broken spirit; a broken and contrite heart you, God, will not despise."*

For believers, humility isn't only about lowering oneself but recognizing the source of all blessings—God. John the Baptist, who had a significant following, consistently pointed to Jesus rather than seek his own glory. In John 3:30, he says, *"He must become greater; I must become less."*

Pride blinds us to our need for God and the truth that everything we have comes from Him. As Proverbs 22:4 says, *"Humility is the fear of the Lord; its wages are riches and honor and life."* **Christ** is the ultimate example of humility. He washed His disciples' feet (John 13:1–17) and willingly went to the cross, showing that true greatness comes from serving others.

In light of these examples, I encourage you to pray for humility. Remember that humility opens the door for God's grace to flow into our lives. Proverbs 3:34 says, *"He mocks proud mockers but shows favor to the humble and oppressed."*

Psalm 149:4 states, *"For the Lord takes delight in his people; he crowns the humble with victory."* I want victory, and because I choose victory, I have to choose humility because they work hands in hands.

Let Proverbs 22:4 be a reminder that true honour and blessing come from walking in humility before God. As we humble ourselves, we acknowledge that every good thing in our lives comes from Him, and we position ourselves to receive His favour and grace.

May we continually seek to embody humility, remembering that God is the source of all our blessings. In our humility, may we find the true honour and life God promises to those who fear Him.

6. Staying connected, abiding in God to bear spiritual fruit. Throughout my spiritual journey, I pray for God to keep me attached to Him, just as branches are attached to a tree, so I can produce the spiritual fruits of His Holy Spirit as outlined in Galatians 5:22–23: *"But the fruit of the Spirit is love, joy, peace, forbearance, kindness, goodness, faithfulness, gentleness and self-control. Against such things there is no law."*

The image of the vine and branches beautifully illustrates this relationship. In John 15:4–5, Jesus says,

> Remain in me, as I also remain in you. No branch can bear fruit by itself; it must remain in the vine. Neither can you bear fruit unless you remain in me. I am the vine; you are the branches. If you remain in me and I in you, you will bear much fruit; apart from me you can do nothing.

Let's unpack the key words in thus passage. The word vine comes from the Old English *wīn*, which refers to the grapevine and by extension a plant's fruit. In Greek, the word is *ámpelos*, symbolizing life and sustenance, just as the vine provides nutrients to the branches.

Therefore, as my God is the tree and I am the branch, as long as I remain attached to the branch I will receive all the nutrients I need. The notion of staying attached is often translated here as the word **abide**, which derives from the Old English *abidan*, meaning to "wait for" or "remain."[5] In the New Testament, the Greek word *ménō* is used to convey the same meaning.

The best way to remain in Him is to dwell in prayer and His Word. Taking this position will help bear fruit.

In this particular situation, the word fruit in Greek is rendered as *karpós*, which also can be translated as either a result or outcome. The fruit of the Spirit therefore refers to the visible results of a life lived in the Spirit.

Let's look at a longer version of this passage:

> I am the vine; you are the branches. If you remain in me and I in you, you will bear much fruit; apart from me you can do nothing. If you do not remain in me, you are like a branch that is thrown away and withers; such branches are picked up, thrown into the fire and burned. If you remain in me and my words remain in you, ask whatever you wish, and it will be done for you. This is to my Father's glory, that you bear much fruit, showing yourselves to be my disciples. (John 15:5–8)

> *Like the branch that withers if it doesn't stay attached to the tree, the same will be true of myself if I stop reading the word of God, communicating with Him in prayer, and growing in relationship with Him.*

Like the branch that withers if it doesn't stay attached to the tree, the same will be true of myself if I stop reading the word of God, communicating with Him in prayer, and growing in relationship with Him.

For Christians, staying connected to Christ (the vine) is essential for spiritual growth and fruitfulness. Just as a branch cannot bear fruit if it is disconnected from the vine, we cannot exhibit the fruits of the Spirit if we aren't rooted in our relationship with

---

[5] "Abide," *Online Etymology Dictionary*. Date of access: December 16, 2024 (https://www.etymonline.com/word/abide).

Jesus. This connection nourishes us spiritually and helps us live in ways that glorify God and bless others.

John 15 also talks about bearing fruit. I usually take the time to pray about the nine fruits of the Holy Spirit, placing emphasis on those which I feel are lacking. It is your call to identify these fruits which you need to produce.

The fruits of the Spirit—love, joy, peace, patience, kindness, goodness, faithfulness, gentleness, and self-control—are the natural outcomes of living in the Spirit. These virtues distinguish believers from unbelievers and serve as a testimony to God's transforming power in our lives. They are not produced by human effort alone but through a deep, abiding relationship with Christ.

Love. This fruit is evident in the life of Ruth, who showed selfless love and loyalty to Naomi (Ruth 1:16–17). Love motivates us to care for others and put their needs before our own. I pray for love every day because I believe it is the most important and difficult fruit to cultivate.

It's easy to overlook the good in people and dwell on their offences. It's so much easier and natural to love those who love me and treat me well. But what about those who hurt, harm, or reject me? Romans 5:8 makes it clear: *"God demonstrates his own love for us in this: while we were still sinners, Christ died for us."* God didn't wait for us to come to Him; He loved us first, despite our flaws.

I have suffered a lot of hurt, abuse, and rejection in my life, so it's not always easy to feel or accept love, let alone love genuinely. But I strive for this kind of love, even though it's a daily struggle. I persevere and pray that God will continue to give me a transfusion of love to enlarge my heart to love as He loves.

How about you?

Joy. Despite his trials, Paul demonstrated joy, rejoicing in the Lord even while in prison (Philippians 4:4). True joy is rooted in God's presence and promises, not circumstances.

Is it hard for you to be joyful regularly? It is for me.

I was astonished the first time I read 1 Thessalonians 5:16, which says, *"Always be joyful"* (CEV). My initial reaction was, "Really? Always?"

Then I began to understand that joy is different from happiness. We are happy when something good happens and unhappy when it doesn't. But joy is a choice. I can choose joy despite my circumstances, and only God can help me reach that level.

What about you?

When I pray for joy, I pray it in two ways, not only to have joy with me but also to carry a contagious joy with me so I can share and brighten other people's days. This is how I would like to be recognized: as a joyful woman, not a grumpy one.

Peace. Jesus is the ultimate example of peace, calming the storm and bringing tranquillity to His disciples (Mark 4:39). Before leaving this world, He reassured His followers with these words from John 14:27 (NKJV): *"Peace I leave with you, My peace I give to you; not as the world gives do I give to you. Let not your heart be troubled, neither let it be afraid."*

Who among us can claim they have never been troubled or afraid in this world? I certainly cannot. As a perfectionist, I struggle with anxiety over even the smallest details, expecting everything to be flawless. I hold high expectations for myself and others, and this perfectionism has caused me great sorrow.

Through Al-Anon's literature, I've come to realize that setting unrealistic goals can lead to frustration and even greater suffering.

The perfectionist, clinging stubbornly to their ideals of how life *ought* to be, often struggles with the concepts of acceptance and detachment. I have often demanded too much of myself and others, trying to play God in my life and theirs. This compulsive drive for perfection has led me to magnify small problems into large ones, deepening my despair when things don't go as planned and making it difficult to accept life as it is.

Throughout my journey with the Lord, I have learned that my search for peace of mind bears fruit more readily when I stop expecting perfection and instead relax into acceptance. Peace is essential for a fulfilled life, and it comes from trusting in God's sovereignty and goodness.

Recently, I've found peace when things don't go as expected. I say, "So God, Your will be done, not mine." I choose not to be upset. I also seek to be an agent of peace wherever I go, bringing the peace of God with me through a peaceful word or hug. I want to be known for that.

And you? How do you infuse peace into your life?

Patience. Job is renowned for his patience during immense suffering, trusting in God's purpose (James 5:11). I also pray for patience, because it is one of my weaknesses. I want to do everything—if not yesterday, then now. Patience is a great virtue; it helps us be still and wait on God's timing. As Hebrews 10:36 reminds us, *"For you have need of endurance, so that after you have done the will of God, you may receive the promise"* (NKJV).

As an achiever, I've often pursued things hastily, trying to force outcomes before their time, and I've faced deep regrets as a result. I once hired an engineer for a construction project. Eager to move forward, I rushed into the agreement and made the first downpayment for their services. I chose this engineer because he had offered the best quote and design, but I didn't take the time to thoroughly evaluate my other options. My impatience cost me dearly. I lost the money, more than $22,000 U.S., and the job was never done. It was a hard lesson.

Now I strive not to hurry. I take my time, asking God to guide me so I can act when the time is right. I still take steps forward, but when doors start to close it serves as a reminder to slow down, re-evaluate, and seek wisdom and discernment. This allows me to wait patiently with grace, though it's never easy.

Is patience a struggle for you too? Patience helps us endure hardships and wait for the right time—God's time.

Kindness. Kindness reflects God's love through practical actions. It's about doing good for others, often stepping out of our way to help, support, or uplift those in need.

Are you genuinely a kind person? At all times? To everyone? I know people who show kindness at work because it's part of their job, but they are rude to their family members.

One day, I overheard someone I respect being extremely rude to a customer service representative who couldn't solve his problem. I had always considered him a model of kindness, so this shocked me and made me reflect on my own shortcomings.

I feel especially challenged when I'm angry, impatient, or sense that someone is taking advantage of me. In those moments, I tend to become defensive and less inclined to show kindness. I need to recognize my triggers so I can pause and prevent myself from saying or doing things I might later regret.

I also know people who find it difficult to be kind when they're in positions of power. They may feel that simply doing favours for others is enough, allowing them to otherwise treat people unkindly because in the belief that their actions justify harsh words or attitudes.

However, this behaviour is not befitting of sons and daughters of the almighty King. God calls us to be kind to everyone, as we are reminded in Ephesians 4:32: *"Be kind to one another, tenderhearted, forgiving one another, as God in Christ forgave you"* (ESV).

Kindness is not a mask we wear when it's convenient. It's not something we can set aside at other times. God requires us to practice kindness at all times, in all circumstances, with everyone.

Think of the good Samaritan who showed kindness by caring for a stranger, providing not only physical assistance but also a generous spirit. The good Samaritan's actions exemplify kindness, showing compassion to a stranger in need (Luke 10:33–34).

Kindness is the proactive expression of compassion—doing something good for someone else. But how do we respond with kindness to those who harm us? It's very difficult, but we must strive for it and ask God for help. I need help. How about you?

Goodness. Goodness involves living out our faith through righteous actions. I strive to live a life of goodness, to reflect God's character in everything I do. However, I know that I fall short at times, letting my own desires get in the way of what is truly good.

Being good isn't only about performing good actions for others. It also involves those situations when we know a certain good would benefit another and we refrain from doing it. How easy it is to refrain from doing something to the ones who hurts us! It's like a way to make them pay. Or perhaps we rejoice from within when those who hurt us stumble. I am guilty of this.

Therefore, I pray daily that God will guide me to do what is right, even when it's not easy, to aim for a good attitude. How do you practice goodness in your life?

Faithfulness. Faithfulness is about remaining true to God and His Word, no matter the circumstances. For me, being faithful is often a challenge, especially when life throws difficulties my way.

It's easy to sing and say that I have faith in God. But when situation turns sour, it's hard for me to trust in God's faithfulness. For instance, one of my little brothers, who was like a son to me, was murdered for his organs. I grieved and blamed everyone, including myself and God. It took me a long time to believe that God was still in control, that I can remain faithful no matter what.

Yet I know that God's faithfulness never wavers. This gives me the strength to stay committed to Him. I ask for God's help to strengthen my faith, even when it's hard. I pray for faithfulness.

How about you? How do you stay faithful in your journey? God can help you stay faithful.

Gentleness. Maybe some wonder about the difference between kindness and gentleness. Gentleness is about the manner in which we approach others, especially in sensitive situations. It's not just what we do, but how we do it.

When Jesus dealt with the woman caught in adultery, He showed gentleness by not condemning her but speaking to her with care and offering grace (John 8:11). Gentleness involves responding with calmness and humility, ensuring that our words and actions don't harm or offend but instead uplift and soothe.

While kindness drives us to act, gentleness guides us in how we carry out those actions, ensuring that they are delivered with love, respect, and care. Gentleness involves humility and care in our interactions with others.

I often struggle with being gentle, especially when I'm frustrated or hurt. But I know that gentleness is a reflection of Christ's love and grace. I pray for a gentle spirit, one that responds to others with kindness and understanding.

Do you find it challenging to be gentle in difficult situations? It can be an area that needs prayer to overcome.

Self-control. Self-control enables us to live according to God's will, even during times of temptation. For me, who has dealt with a lot of abuse, I have felt much anger. This is why it's an ongoing battle to exercise self-control. Whether it's controlling my emotions, words, or actions, I often find myself falling short.

But I know that self-control is crucial for living a life that honours God. I pray for the strength to resist temptation and choose God's way over my own desires.

How do you practice self-control in your life?

Praying for the fruits of the Spirit is essential because it aligns our desires with God's will. By asking God to cultivate these fruits in our lives, we acknowledge our dependence on Him and invite His transformative power to work within us.

In Galatians 5:16–17, Paul writes, *"So I say, walk by the Spirit, and you will not gratify the desires of the flesh. For the flesh desires what is contrary to the Spirit, and the Spirit what is contrary to the flesh."* Praying for these fruits helps us to walk by the Spirit, resisting the desires of the flesh and growing in godliness.

Let us pray for these virtues to flourish in our lives, that we may reflect Christ's character and bring glory to God in all we do.

7. Growing faith, trusting God to move mountains. Faith isn't just a word; it's the foundation of our relationship with God. Hebrews 11:6 reminds us that *"without faith it is impossible to please God, because anyone who comes to him must believe that he exists and that he rewards those who earnestly seek him."*

I long to please God, to receive the reward of pleasing Him, and to have a faith that can move mountains, just as my Father promised in Matthew 17:20–21: *"Truly I tell you, if you have faith as small as a mustard seed, you can say to this mountain, 'Move from here to there,' and it will move. Nothing will be impossible for you."*

The mustard seed is one of the smallest seeds known, yet Jesus used it to illustrate the immense power of even the smallest amount of faith. That mustard seed, though tiny, grows into a large tree. Similarly, even a small, seemingly insignificant faith, when nurtured, can grow into something powerful and life-changing.

When Jesus spoke of faith moving mountains, He used a powerful metaphor. A mountain is an obstacle that seems impossible to overcome. But with faith, even the largest obstacles can be removed.

You might say that you've never seen a mountain literally move, and that's true. In the spiritual sense, however, I have witnessed how faith can move the proverbial mountains in our lives—the challenges, hardships, and impossible situations that seem insurmountable.

I wasn't born with a silver spoon in my mouth. My life has been a struggle from the very beginning. As a baby, I faced abuse from a close family member and my journey has been filled with challenges ever since.

But when I came to know the Lord and started walking with Him, everything began to change. Little by little, he opened doors no one else could open and closed doors that needed to be closed. My faith has moved mountains in my life.

After earning my MBA, I chose to return to my home country to give back to my community. However, when the situation in my country deteriorated and it became unsafe to live there, I prayed for God to open doors for my family to legally emigrate.

That's when I crossed paths with David Katz, the CEO of Plastic Bank Recycling Corporation, marking the beginning of my journey with his company. And seven years later, amidst dire safety challenges, God answered my prayers. When Plastic Bank's operations in my country were shut down, David served as God's instrument, opening an unexpected door of opportunity. He offered me a new position in Vancouver and provided a fresh start for my family and me.

David was a response to my prayers, just as Proverbs 21:1 reminds us: *"The king's heart is in the hand of the Lord, like the rivers of water; He turns it wherever He wishes"* (NKJV). This experience also reflects the truth of God's promise in Jeremiah 29:11: *"'For I know the plans I have for you,' declares the Lord, 'plans to prosper you and not to harm you, plans to give you hope and a future.'"*

Through this journey, I learned that having faith in God is essential. Yet it's not merely about the size of my faith but the greatness of the One in whom I have placed my faith. God's faithfulness and ability to bring hope and purpose, even in the most challenging circumstances, remain constant and true.

There is a deep connection between having faith and being faithful. Faith is our trust in God, believing in His promises and His ability to move the mountains in our lives. But being faithful means living out that trust every day, consistently obeying and serving God in the small things as well as the big things.

Matthew 25:21 says, *"Well done, good and faithful servant! You have been faithful with a few things; I will put you in charge of many things. Come and share your master's happiness!"* This verse highlights the reward of faithfulness. A faithful servant is one who has great faith—not just in words, but in action. In addition to believing in God's promises, such a person lives in a way that reflects that belief.

Every day, I pray that my faith will grow larger than the faith I had yesterday. Faith isn't static; it's meant to grow, just like the mustard seed. And as our faith grows, so does our faithfulness. We become more consistent in our walk with God, more committed to His purposes, and more confident in His promises.

So I encourage you to pray for your faith to grow, too. Ask God to help you trust Him more, to believe in His power to move the mountains in your life. But also pray for the strength to be faithful in the small things, to serve Him with all your heart and remain steadfast in your commitment to Him. As we grow in faith and faithfulness, we will see God do amazing things in our lives, far beyond what we could ask for or imagine.

8. Seeking wisdom, the gift of discernment. Wisdom and discernment are spiritual gifts that enable us to make sound decisions and distinguish between what is good and what is best.

Wisdom is the ability to apply knowledge and understanding in practical ways, making choices that align with God's will. Discernment, on the other hand, is the ability to perceive and distinguish between right and wrong, truth and falsehood, good and evil. Together, these gifts guide us through life's complexities, helping us navigate difficult decisions and avoid pitfalls.

Have you ever found yourself in a situation where you had to choose between two seemingly good options, and it was difficult to determine which was best? I have, and it's challenging, especially when the decision eventually involves emotions that can lead to great regret. In such moments, wisdom and discernment are invaluable. They protect us from making decisions that may seem right in the moment but later lead to undesirable consequences.

I once shared with my dear friend Bryce, who has since passed away, that if I were offered any superpower in real life, I would choose the ability to know the future. His response was that this sounded scary! Yes, it might be frightening to know with certainty what the future holds, but I felt that having such knowledge would empower me to plan and act accordingly.

However, the reality is that we don't need to know the future when we trust in God's wisdom and discernment. He knows the future and these gifts empower us to trust His guidance and choose the best path, even when the future is uncertain.

The story of King Solomon provides a powerful example of the importance of wisdom. In 1 Kings 3:5–14, God appeared to Solomon in a dream and offered him anything he desired. Instead of asking for wealth, long life, or victory over his enemies, Solomon asked for wisdom to govern his people well. His request pleased God because it demonstrated a selfless concern for others and a desire to serve Him faithfully. As a result, God not only granted Solomon wisdom but also blessed him with riches and honour:

> Then God said to him: "Because you have asked this thing, and have not asked long life for yourself, nor have asked riches for yourself, nor have asked the life of your enemies, but have asked for yourself understanding to discern justice, behold, I have done according to your words; see, I have given you a wise and understanding heart, so that there has not been anyone like you before you, nor shall any like you arise after you. (1 Kings 3:11–12, NKJV)

Awesome! I want that. How about you?

Solomon's story teaches us that when our priorities align with God's will, He blesses us beyond what we could ever imagine. It reminds us that seeking God's wisdom and guidance should be our foremost interest, and He will take care of the rest.

The Bible is filled with verses that highlight the importance of wisdom and discernment. Proverbs 2:6–7 says, *"For the Lord gives wisdom; from his mouth come knowledge and understanding. He holds success in store for the upright, he is a shield to those whose walk is blameless."* True wisdom comes from God, and when we seek it He provides protection and success.

James 1:5 also encourages us to seek wisdom: *"If any of you lacks wisdom, you should ask God, who gives generously to all without finding fault, and it will be given to you."* This promise assures us that God is willing and eager to grant us wisdom when we ask for it in faith.

Discernment is equally important. Philippians 1:9–10 says,

> And this is my prayer: that your love may abound more and more in knowledge and depth of insight, so that you may be able to discern what is best and may be pure and blameless for the day of Christ...

Discernment helps us choose what is best and live a life that is pleasing to God.

As we navigate life's challenges, it's crucial to pray for wisdom and discernment. These gifts help us make decisions that honour God and protect us from falling into evil. They enable us to see beyond the surface and recognize the true nature of things. By seeking God's wisdom and discernment, we allow Him to guide our steps, ensuring that we remain on the path He has set for us.

So I encourage you to make wisdom and discernment a priority in your prayers. Ask God to fill you with His wisdom, help you discern between what is good and what is best, and protect you from the schemes of the enemy. As we grow in these gifts, we will find ourselves making decisions that lead to life, peace, and blessings, both for ourselves and those around us.

9. Spiritual armour, embracing the battleground, not the playground. This prayer essential serves as a crucial reminder that this life is not a playground. It is a battlefield, and we are soldiers in God's army.

When I chose to follow Jesus, I also committed to taking up my cross and following Him, as He instructs in Luke 9:23: *"If anyone would come after Me, let him deny himself, and take up his cross daily, and follow Me"* (NKJV). This call to take up the cross isn't easy. It requires us to die to self and live for Christ.

We must remember that we are at war and our enemy is real, as 1 Peter 5:8 warns us: *"Be alert and of sober mind. Your enemy the devil prowls around like a roaring lion looking for someone to devour."*

My life has felt like a constant fight, whether it's battling character flaws or striving to have my voice heard. Embracing life often means fighting to thrive where we are planted. Therefore, I need to be vigilant and stand my ground.

As a warrior in God's army, I must be equipped with the right tools for battle. Ephesians 6:11–12 instructs us,

> Put on the full armor of God, so that you can take your stand against the devil's schemes. For our struggle is not against flesh and blood, but against the rulers, against the authorities, against the powers of this dark world and against the spiritual forces of evil in the heavenly realms.

This passage reminds me that our battle is not against people but against spiritual forces of evil. Thus, it is essential to wear the spiritual armour daily and pray for each piece as listed in Ephesians 6:13–17:

> Therefore put on the full armor of God, so that when the day of evil comes, you may be able to stand your ground, and after you have done everything, to stand. Stand firm then, with the belt of truth buckled around your waist, with the breastplate of righteousness in place, and with your feet fitted with the readiness that

comes from the gospel of peace. In addition to all this, take up the shield of faith, with which you can extinguish all the flaming arrows of the evil one. Take the helmet of salvation and the sword of the Spirit, which is the word of God.

Let's unpack each offensive and defensive piece armour we have been equipped with to fight in this spiritual war.

The belt of truth. The apostle Paul urges us to *"be strong in the Lord and in his mighty power"* (Ephesians 6:10). This is key to understanding the armour of God. Each piece—truth, righteousness, the gospel, faith, and salvation—comes from God and is given to us for our defence. All except *"the sword of the Spirit, which is the word of God"* (Ephesians 6:17), are defensive in nature, designed to help us *"stand against the devil's schemes"* (Ephesians 6:11).

The belt of truth is listed first because without truth we are lost and the devil's schemes will overpower us. The belt of truth holds everything together.

In Roman armour, the belt was essential for securing the soldier's tunic and holding his weapons. Spiritually, the belt of truth represents the truth of God's Word, which holds our lives together and prepares us for battle.

As believers, we must wrap ourselves in truth, rejecting the lies of the enemy. Jesus declared, *"I am the way and the truth and the life"* (John 14:6). This truth is the foundation upon which we stand firm against deception and falsehood.

The first great sin, according to God's Word, was a lie. The enemy used a lie to deceive Eve, and he has been using lies ever since. People have told me lies from a young age. As a frank and direct person, I have always tried my best to speak the truth, even when it's uncomfortable. I don't like to be lied to and I aim not to lie either.

That said, I cannot claim that I have never lied.

One of the greatest compliments I've ever received came indirectly from my spouse. I overheard him speaking on the phone one day when he thought I was not home. He said, "My wife is not perfect—nobody is—but one thing I know for sure is she will not blatantly lie to you. If anything, she might hurt you by telling you the truth bluntly."

I took that as a compliment.

This brings me to an important distinction between telling a lie and choosing to remain silent. The story about Saul in 1 Samuel 10 illustrates this well. After being anointed king by the prophet Samuel, Saul returned home and met his uncle, who asked what Samuel had told him. Saul truthfully mentioned that Samuel had informed him that the donkeys were found, but he chose to say nothing about being anointed king. Saul's decision to withhold that information wasn't deceitful; it demonstrated discernment and wisdom about what should and should not be shared.

Jesus Himself showed this principle in His ministry. After performing miracles, He sometimes instructed people not to tell anyone. For instance, in Mark 1:44, after healing a man with leprosy, Jesus said to him, *"See that you don't tell this to anyone. But go, show yourself to the priest and offer the sacrifices that Moses commanded for your cleansing, as a testimony to them."* This shows us that silence can serve a purpose; it's not inherently deceitful.

In my own life, I have encountered situations when remaining silent was not only wise but also necessary for my protection.

For example, my younger brother was kidnapped at the age of ten and narrowly escaped death. In my home country, it is tragically common for the same individual to be kidnapped more than once. If someone were to ask where my brother lived, I would absolutely keep that information private to protect him from harm.

In such a case, withholding the truth isn't lying. It's exercising wisdom to safeguard another's life.

This reminds me of the story of Rahab in the book of Joshua, which presents a unique and challenging case. As a woman living in Jericho, Rahab played a crucial role in the Israelites' conquest of the city. In Joshua 2, she hid the Israelite spies and lied to the king's men about their whereabouts. This act of deception was pivotal in protecting the spies and securing the Israelites' victory, leading to Rahab and her family's salvation when Jericho fell. Rahab is even honoured in the genealogy of Jesus Christ, as mentioned in Matthew 1:5.

At first glance, it may seem contradictory to include Rahab's story in a discussion about truth, as she used deception to achieve a righteous outcome. However, this story challenges us to look deeper into the complexities of truth and deception in God's plan.

Rahab's actions raise important questions. Was it wrong for her to lie? How does her story align with the Bible's teachings about truth and lies? These are not easy questions, and they invite us to explore the broader context of God's grace and the complexities of human morality.

The belt of truth represents the truth of God's Word, which is foundational to our spiritual defence. Yet Rahab's lie led to the preservation of life and the fulfillment of God's plan for His people. This doesn't mean that lying is condoned by God. Rather, it highlights that He can work through imperfect people and situations to bring about His purposes.

Rahab's story teaches us that God values the heart's intention and the outcome that aligns with His will. Rahab's lie was not celebrated; her faith and courage were. She recognized the truth of God's power and aligned herself with His people, even at great personal risk. Hebrews 11:31 commends Rahab for her faith, not her deception.

As believers, we are called to live in truth, speak the truth, and stand firm in the truth of God's Word. However, Rahab's story reminds us that God's grace is greater than our shortcomings and His plans are far beyond our understanding. It challenges us to trust in God's sovereignty, knowing that He can redeem even our flawed actions when we act in faith and align our hearts with His will.

In spiritual warfare, the belt of truth is essential for holding everything together. Just as a Roman soldier's belt secured his armour and held his weapons, the truth of God's Word secures our spiritual lives and prepares us for battle. Yet we also see through Rahab's story that God's truth is not always simple or straightforward. It is deeply rooted in His grace, mercy, and the greater good of His kingdom.

Let us, therefore, strive to live by the truth, acknowledging that while our actions may be imperfect, our faith and alignment with God's will can lead to redemption and fulfillment of His promises. May we pray to always wear the belt of truth, not just in our words but in our hearts and intentions, trusting in God's wisdom and grace to guide us in all circumstances.

Unfortunately, through my own experience, the world has taught me that I should be more diplomatic. I have learned that a white lie can be okay. But I've also learned that when I cannot speak the truth, it is better to remain silent—unless it is for the greater good, as was the case with Rahab. It is important to understand the roots and reasons behind lies. Lies have nearly destroyed my life, and I know firsthand the pain of being deceived.

Someone I dearly loved once lied to me about a very important matter. That lie destroyed a marriage, fractured many families, and deeply hurt those who loved him. The repercussions of that lie still affect many today.

As John 8:44 states,

> You belong to your father, the devil, and you want to carry out your father's desires. He was a murderer from the beginning, not holding to the truth, for there is no truth in him. When he lies, he speaks his native language, for he is a liar and the father of lies.

Have you ever wondered how much better the world would be if everyone spoke the truth? Some people lie about everything, even small details, until they start to believe their lies are the truth.

Another form of lying is hiding the truth. Some convince themselves that they are simply being private, but this often serves to cover up lies.

Lies thrive in secrecy, encouraging darkness and deceit, while truth is compared to light, which cannot be hidden. We read in Luke 8:16–18,

> No one lights a lamp and then covers it with a washtub or shoves it under the bed. No, you set it up on a lamp stand so those who enter the room can see their way. We're not keeping secrets; we're telling them. We're not

hiding things; we're bringing everything out into the open. (MSG)

Is someone in your life trying to conceal something? Perhaps their relationship with you? If so, that could be a sign of deception. Beware and step out of the darkness.

I know many who have suffered because of lies, unable to live in a fulfilled and open manner due to the falsehoods told about them.

It is no accident that truth is depicted as a belt around our waist. Just as a strong waist is necessary for standing and fighting, so is the belt of truth essential in spiritual warfare. As long as we choose to live in lies, we cannot effectively fight the enemy, for he is the prince of lies.

Jesus used the truth of God's Word to combat Satan's lies during His temptation in the wilderness (Matthew 4:1–11). Each time Satan tempted Him, Jesus responded with scripture, showing us the importance of knowing and using the truth in spiritual warfare. How well do you know the Word of God, the truth that empowers you to fight the prince of lies? Do you hold yourself accountable in your speech, ensuring that you always tell the truth? I do.

I pray that God will help me always wear the belt of truth, to live in the truth, speak the truth, and stand firm in the truth of His Word. How about you?

The breastplate of righteousness. The imagery here is of an armed Roman or Israelite soldier, prepared for battle. A typical soldier's breastplate, made of bronze or chainmail, covered the vital organs, especially the heart, and was secured by loops or buckles attached to a thick belt. If the belt was loosened, the breastplate would slip off.

When Paul compares the armour of God to military gear, each piece symbolizes a part of God's strength extended to us as His children. The breastplate of righteousness refers to the righteousness purchased for us by Jesus at the cross (2 Corinthians 5:21).

At salvation, this breastplate is issued to every repentant sinner, specially designed by God to protect our heart and soul from evil and deception. Our own righteous acts are insufficient against Satan's attacks (Isaiah 64:6). The breastplate of righteousness has Christ's name stamped on it, as though He says, "Your righteousness isn't enough to protect you. Wear mine."

We are instructed to put on this armour, which implies that it isn't automatically worn all the time. Putting on the armour of God requires a conscious decision on our part. To put on the breastplate of righteousness, we must first ensure that the belt of truth is firmly in place. Without truth, our righteousness will be based on our own efforts to impress God, leading to legalism or self-condemnation (Romans 8:1). Instead we must acknowledge that apart from Him we can do nothing (John 15:5). We must see ourselves as being in Christ, knowing that despite our failures His righteousness has been credited to our account.

We put on this breastplate by seeking God and His righteousness above all else (Matthew 6:33). We make Him and His ways our dwelling place (Psalm 91:1). We delight in His commands and desire for His ways to become our ways (Psalm 37:4, 119:24, 111, Isaiah 61:10). When God reveals an area in need of change, we obey and allow Him to work in us. If we say no to God, we create a crack in our armour through which Satan's arrows can penetrate (Ephesians 6:16).

As we wear Christ's breastplate of righteousness, we develop a purity of heart that translates into righteous action. Wearing this breastplate leads to a lifestyle wherein our beliefs align with our actions. As our lives conform to the image of Christ (Romans 8:29), our choices become more righteous, and these godly choices protect us from further temptation and deception (Proverbs 8:20, Psalm 23:3).

However, if we abuse or wear the armour incorrectly, it can malfunction. Similarly, factors like carelessness (1 Peter 5:8), unbelief (Hebrews 3:12), abusing grace (Romans 6:1-2), or disobedience (1 John 3:4, Hebrews 4:6) can hinder our ability to stand firm and defeat the enemy. When we tolerate sin, refuse to forgive (2 Corinthians 2:10-11), rely on our own righteousness (Titus 3:5), or allow worldly concerns to crowd out time with God, we effectively remove the breastplate of righteousness, minimizing its protective power.

We need our breastplate of righteousness securely in place to gain the victory described in 2 Corinthians 10:5: *"We demolish arguments and every pretension that sets itself up against the knowledge of God, and we take captive every thought to make it obedient to Christ."* When we reject heretical ideas, idolatry, and the *"counsel of the ungodly"* (Psalm 1:1, NKJV), and instead *"looking unto Jesus, the author and finisher of our faith"* (Hebrews 12:2, NKJV), we ensure that our breastplate is fastened.

The breastplate is vital for protecting the heart, the centre of our spiritual lives. The breastplate of righteousness represents the righteousness we receive through faith in Christ, guarding our hearts against the enemy's accusations and condemnations. It is not our own righteousness, but the righteousness of Christ imputed to us through faith.

Have you ever felt that you need to do more for God to accept you, perhaps by attending church more frequently, paying more tithes, or performing acts of kindness for others to see? I have. But I need to remind myself that God's mercy and grace cannot be earned. As Ephesians 2:8–10 says,

> For by grace you have been saved through faith, and that not of yourselves; it is the gift of God, not of works, lest anyone should boast. For we are His workmanship, created in Christ Jesus for good works, which God prepared beforehand that we should walk in them. (NKJV)

I don't have to work to be righteous before God. I know people who judge themselves or others for missing a day of worship, forgetting that the true place of worship is within us. Wherever God plants us, to be the salt of the earth and the light of the world, that is our place of worship. Going to church doesn't make me more righteous than those who don't attend. We fellowship to be able to meet one another and encourage one another as we are told in Hebrews 10:25: *"not giving up meeting together, as some are in the habit of doing, but encouraging one another—and all the more as you see the Day approaching."* Our righteousness is demonstrated through our obedience, which protects us. Hence it is compared to a breastplate.

Let us remember Joseph, who demonstrated righteousness by resisting the advances of Potiphar's wife (Genesis 39). He chose to honour God rather than give in to sin, even when it meant suffering unjustly.

Isaiah 59:17 describes God putting on righteousness as His breastplate, showing that righteousness is an essential part of our spiritual defence. Righteousness is defensive armour, not offensive. We choose to keep ourselves right in our actions and motivations, but God has already made us righteous through Jesus Christ.

I pray that God will cover me with the breastplate of righteousness, protecting my heart from the enemy's attacks and helping me to live a life that reflects His righteousness.

How about you? I invite you to do the same.

The gospel of peace. Our feet carry us into battle, and they must be fitted with the readiness that comes from the gospel of peace. This means being prepared to share the good news of Jesus Christ at all times.

The gospel of peace brings reconciliation between God and humanity and enables us to stand firm against the chaos and turmoil of this world. This armour reminds me of the great commission we have all received. In Matthew 28:18–20, Jesus says,

> All authority in heaven and on earth has been given to me. Therefore go and make disciples of all nations, baptizing them in the name of the Father and of the Son and of the Holy Spirit, and teaching them to obey everything I have commanded you. And surely I am with you always, to the very end of the age.

The word readiness implies constant vigilance. A victorious soldier must be prepared for battle. He must have studied his enemy's strategy, be confident in his own strategy, and have his feet firmly planted to hold his ground when the attack comes. A soldier's shoes were studded with nails or spikes, like cleats, to help him keep his balance in combat. He knew that if he lost his footing and went down, it wouldn't matter how great the rest of his armour was; the enemy would have him.

When we are ready with the gospel of peace, we live with the understanding that we are continually under attack from Satan. As 2 Timothy 4:2 says, *"Preach the word; be ready in season and out of season…"*

These shoes of peace that God supplies His soldiers have two purposes: defensive and offensive. To defend ourselves against the *"flaming arrows of the evil one"* (Ephesians 6:16), we must have confidence in our position in Christ. We must stand firm in the truth of God's Word, regardless of how terrifying the circumstances may be (1 John 5:14). We must understand grace without abusing it (Romans 6:1–6), remember that our position in Christ isn't based on our abilities or worthiness (Titus 3:5), and keep our belt of truth and breastplate of righteousness securely fastened (2 Timothy 1:12).

When Satan attacks with a missile of doubt, such as implying that God wouldn't have let calamity befall us if He really loved us—as he did with me when my little brother was murdered—I have to dig my shoes of peace into the turf of God's Word and reply that *"all things work together for the good to those who love God, to those who are called according to His purpose"* (Romans 8:28, NKJV).

When Satan stabs from behind by saying, "Remember what you did?" I dig in more deeply and reply, *"If we confess our sins, He is faithful and just to forgive us our sins and to cleanse us from all unrighteousness"* (1 John 1:9, NKJV). And instead of coming out bitter and regretful, like Judas Iscariot, I come out victorious through repentance.

In addition to standing our ground, shoes are also meant for moving. God expects us to go on the offensive and take the gospel of peace to others. We read in 1 Peter 3:15, *"Always be prepared to give an answer to everyone who asks you to give the reason for the hope that you have."*

Sharing our faith is one of the best ways to maintain our own sure footing. God knows that when we are active in speaking of Him to others, we not only charge into Satan's territory but dig our shoes more deeply into truth and make ourselves harder to dislodge. When you *"present yourself to God as one approved"* (2 Timothy 2:15, NKJV), you are ready to stand firm in the gospel of peace, no matter what the enemy brings against you (2 Thessalonians 2:15).

Are you sharing the gospel of peace in your way of being, in your attitude, and by being the light of the world and salt of the earth?

The apostle Paul is an excellent example of someone who had his feet fitted with the readiness of the gospel. He travelled extensively, preaching the gospel and bringing peace to those who were far from God (Acts 13:47). I admire those who have received the gift of being an evangelist, which requires great courage and boldness. Praise God, for when He sends us out into the world, He also equips us.

However, we are all evangelists, having received the call of the great commission. Maybe this book is ministering to you the gospel of God. Perhaps you are ministering the gospel to those who know you in different ways. Romans 10:15 says, *"How beautiful are the feet of those who preach the gospel of peace..."* (NKJV) This highlights the importance of being ready to share the gospel wherever we go.

I pray that God will equip my feet with the readiness that comes from the gospel of peace so I may stand firm and be a messenger of His peace wherever He sends me. How about you?

The shield of faith. The shield of faith is our defence against the flaming arrows of the evil one. Faith is our trust and confidence in God, and it protects us from the enemy's attacks. When doubt, fear, and temptation come our way, our faith in God's promises acts as a shield, guarding us from spiritual harm.

Hebrews 11:1 defines faith as *"the substance of things hoped for, the evidence of things not seen."* Faith is essential in our spiritual battle, enabling us to trust in God's unseen hand at work in our lives.

After summarizing the gospel in his epistle to the Ephesians and giving various instructions, Paul concludes by saying, *"Finally, be strong in the Lord and in his mighty power. Put on the full armor of God, so that you can take your stand against the devil's schemes"* (Ephesians 6:10–11). Regarding the shield, Paul writes, *"In addition to all this, take up the shield of faith, with which you can extinguish all the flaming arrows of the evil one"* (Ephesians 6:16). The English Standard Version emphasizes this differently: *"In all circumstances take up the shield of faith, with which you can extinguish all the flaming darts of the evil one..."* (ESV)

A shield is vitally important to a soldier, providing a blanket of protection. It is meant to be taken up in all circumstances, serving as the first barrier against the enemy's attack. Often shields were painted with identifying marks; a Christian who takes up the shield of faith identifies himself as a foot soldier in the Lord's army (Joshua 5:14).

Hebrews 11:6 stresses the importance of faith: *"And without faith it is impossible to please God…"* Satan's attacks can sometimes cause us to doubt God, but faith prompts us to believe Him. We give in to temptation when we believe that what he offers is better than what God has promised. Faith reminds us that although God's promise may not be immediately visible, He is true to His Word. When Satan attempts to plague us with doubt or entice us with instant gratification, like he did with Eve, faith recognizes the deceptiveness of his tactics and quickly extinguishes the arrows. When Satan accuses us, faith chooses to believe that Jesus has redeemed us and there is no more condemnation (Romans 8:1, 34, Revelation 12:10–12).

Faith is one of the greatest gifts (1 Corinthians 13:13), and it is the means by which we receive grace and come into right relationship with God (Ephesians 2:8–9). Because we have been justified through faith, we belong to God and have peace with Him (Romans 5:1). Faith is the doorway to hope in God (Romans 5:2). Because we have faith in God, our suffering need not faze us; in fact, we can persevere through it (Romans 5:3–5).

All believers have this promise: *"everyone born of God overcomes the world. This is the victory that has overcome the world, even our faith"* (1 John 5:4). Faith is a protective barrier between us and the schemes of Satan. When we believe God and take Him at His Word, we remain grounded in truth. Then the lies of the enemy lose their power and we become overcomers. In this way, faith is our shield.

Shadrach, Meshach, and Abednego demonstrated the shield of faith when they refused to bow to King Nebuchadnezzar's idol, trusting that God would deliver them from the fiery furnace (Daniel 3).

I pray that God will strengthen my faith so I may use it as a shield to extinguish the flaming arrows of doubt, fear, and temptation that the enemy sends my way. I invite you to use your faith as a shield of protection.

The helmet of salvation. The helmet of salvation protects our minds, which are often the primary battleground in spiritual warfare. It represents the assurance of our salvation in Christ, guarding our thoughts from doubt and despair. When we are confident in our salvation and secure in Christ, we can stand firm against the enemy's lies and accusations. The apostle Peter exemplified the helmet of salvation when he boldly proclaimed the gospel after Pentecost, despite threats and persecution from the authorities (Acts 4:19–20).

Ephesians 6:17 instructs us to put on the whole armour of God, including *"the helmet of salvation and the sword of the Spirit, which is the word of God."* In ancient times, when a soldier suited up for battle, the helmet was the last piece of armour to be put on, symbolizing the final act of readiness for combat. The helmet was vital for survival, protecting the brain, the command centre of the body. If the head was damaged, the rest of the armour would be of little use.

The assurance of salvation is our impenetrable defence against anything the enemy throws at us. Jesus said, *"Do not be afraid of those who kill the body but cannot kill the soul. Rather, be afraid of the One who can destroy both soul and body in hell"* (Matthew 10:28). This is a reminder that as we prepare for Satan's attacks, we must firmly secure our helmet of salvation.

Salvation isn't just a one-time event or future hope; it's an ongoing, eternal state that we, as God's children, enjoy in the present. It provides daily protection and deliverance from our sinful nature and Satan's schemes. This is why, although I have been saved, I renew my commitment every day through prayer, the same way married couples renew their vows. Even though my perfect heavenly Father never changes—He is the same yesterday, today, and tomorrow—I do change. Therefore, I want to check regularly that I'm changing toward Him, not away from Him.

Because of the power of the cross, our enemy no longer has any hold on us (Romans 6:10, 8:2, 1 Corinthians 1:18). While Satan is aware of this, he knows that many of God's children are not, or at least they do not live as if they are. We must keep our helmets securely fastened so his fiery darts don't penetrate our thoughts and set us on a destructive path. Through the helmet of salvation, we can *"demolish arguments and every pretension that sets itself up against the knowledge of God, and we take captive every thought to make it obedient to Christ"* (2 Corinthians 10:5).

To keep this helmet fastened and functioning, believers can take several actions.

First, we can renew our minds. Our minds are battlefields, and the outcomes of those battles determine the course of our lives. Romans 12:1–2 instructs us to renew our minds by allowing the truth of God's Word to replace anything that runs contrary to it. Old ideas, opinions, and worldviews must be replaced with God's truth, which washes away the world's filth, lies, and confusion.

Next, reject doubts that arise from circumstances. As sensory creatures, we tend to disregard what we cannot perceive with our five senses. Circumstances may tempt us to believe that God doesn't love us or that His Word isn't true.

James 3:11 asks, *"Can both fresh water and salt water flow from the same spring?"* It is impossible to have faith and doubt simultaneously. With the helmet of salvation firmly in place, we can choose to believe in what seems impossible (Hebrews 11:6, 1 Peter 1:8–9).

It's also wise to keep an eternal perspective. When life becomes overwhelming, we must remember to look up. Our salvation is the most precious gift we have received, and keeping our eyes on this fact can help us weather life's storms. We can live by the motto "If it doesn't have eternal significance, it's not that important."

My perfectionist tendencies once led me to place high demands on my spouse. I needed him to love me in a specific way, aligned with my own love language. I had to hit an emotional low to realize an important truth: my spouse, as a human being with free will, may never fully express love in the exact way I desire. This realization brought me to a place of surrender. I had to turn to God, who alone can love me perfectly and unconditionally.

While my spouse's choice not to fully embrace my love language can cause pain and strain on our marriage, I have come to understand that it lacks eternal significance. This shift in perspective has freed me from misplaced expectations, allowing me to adjust my mindset and find peace in God's perfect love.

As 2 Corinthians 4:18 reminds us: *"So we fix our eyes not on what is seen, but on what is unseen, since what is seen is temporary, but what is unseen is eternal."* This verse has helped me focus on the eternal reality of God's love rather than being consumed by temporary disappointments in human relationships.

Remember that victory is already accomplished. When we consider ourselves *"dead to sin but alive to God"* (Romans 6:11), we eliminate many opportunities for Satan to entrap us. When we recognize ourselves as new creatures (2 Corinthians 5:17, 1 John 3:9), choosing sin is no longer an option.

Finally, we should find our hope in Him. As Psalm 73:25 says, *"Whom have I in heaven but you? And earth has nothing I desire besides you."*

Our helmet is most effective when we treasure what it represents. The salvation Jesus purchased for us cannot share the place of importance in our hearts with earthly things. When pleasing the Lord is our supreme delight, we eliminate many of Satan's lures and render his evil suggestions powerless.

As we wear the helmet of salvation daily, our minds become more insulated against the enemy's suggestions and traps. We choose to guard our minds from excessive worldly influence and instead focus on things that honour Christ (Philippians 4:8). In doing so, our salvation becomes a protective helmet that *"will guard our hearts and minds in Christ Jesus"* (Philippians 4:7).

We read in 1 Thessalonians 5:8, *"But let us who are of the day be sober, putting on the breastplate of faith and love, and as a helmet the hope of salvation"* (NKJV). The hope of our salvation protects our minds from the enemy's attacks.

I pray that God will place the helmet of salvation on my head, protecting my mind from doubt, fear, and despair, and fill me with the assurance of my salvation in Christ. And I pray this over your life as well.

The sword of the spirit. The sword of the Spirit is the only offensive weapon in the armour of God, representing the Word of God, which is *"living and powerful, and sharper than any two-edged sword"* (Hebrews 4:12, NKJV).

The Word of God is powerful in defeating the enemy and exposing his lies. When we know and use Scripture, we can counter the enemy's attacks and stand firm in the truth. As Psalm 119:105 declares, *"Your word is a lamp for my feet, a light on my path."* The Word of God not only guides us in our spiritual battle but illuminates the path of righteousness.

Scripture only references the sword of the Spirit once, but it is one of the essential pieces of spiritual armour Paul urges the Ephesian Christians to put on as part of the armour of God, enabling us to stand firm against evil (Ephesians 6:13).

The sword serves both offensive and defensive purposes for a soldier. In this case, it is a weapon belonging to the Holy Spirit. Swords were used to protect oneself from harm or to attack the enemy. In both scenarios, rigid training was essential for a soldier to use the sword effectively, ensuring maximum protection and impact.

Similarly, all Christian soldiers need rigorous training to know how to wield the sword of the Spirit, which is Scripture. As 2 Timothy 3:16–17 tells us, the Word of God is divinely inspired by the Holy Spirit and written by men. Since every Christian is engaged in a spiritual battle with the satanic forces of this world, it is crucial that we learn how to handle the Word properly. Only then will it serve as an effective defence against evil and an offensive weapon to destroy strongholds of error and falsehood (2 Corinthians 10:4–5).

God describes the Word as living, active, and sharper than a double-edged sword (Hebrews 4:12). The Roman sword, commonly made with two edges, was designed to penetrate easily and cut in every direction. The Word of God reaches the proverbial heart, the very core of our actions, and lays bare the motives and feelings of those it touches.

The purpose of the sword of the Spirit, the Bible, is to make us strong and able to withstand the onslaughts of Satan, our enemy (Psalm 119:11, 33–40, 99–105). The Holy Spirit uses the power of the Word to save souls and give them the spiritual strength to become mature soldiers for the Lord, equipped to fight in this corrupt world. The more we know and understand the Word of God, the more effective we will be in doing the will of God and in standing against the enemy of our souls.

Jesus Himself used the sword of the Spirit when He was tempted by Satan in the wilderness. Each time Satan tempted Him, Jesus responded with Scripture, cutting through the enemy's lies with the truth of God's Word (Matthew 4:1–11).

I pray that God will equip me with the sword of the Spirit so I may use it to counter the enemy's attacks and stand firm in the truth. I also encourage you to pray over your own life.

Praying in the Spirit on all occasions. Prayer is the power that activates the armour of God. Through prayer, we put on the armour and stand firm against the enemy. Praying in the Spirit means aligning our prayers with God's will, allowing the Holy Spirit to guide and intercede for us. It is essential in our spiritual battle, as it connects us with God's power and enables us to stand strong.

> *Prayer is the power that activates the armour of God. Through prayer, we put on the armour and stand firm against the enemy.*

The early church demonstrated the power of prayer when they fervently prayed for Peter's release from prison, and God answered their prayers by sending an angel to free him (Acts 12:5–11).

Praying in the Spirit is mentioned three times in Scripture:

> So what shall I do? I will pray with my spirit, but I will also pray with my understanding; I will sing with my spirit, but I will also sing with my understanding. (1 Corinthians 14:15)

> And pray in the Spirit on all occasions with all kinds of prayers and requests. With this in mind, be alert and always keep on praying for all the Lord's people. (Ephesians 6:18)

> But you, dear friends, by building yourselves up in your most holy faith and praying in the Holy Spirit...
> (Jude 20)

So what does it mean to pray in the Spirit?

The Greek word translated here as pray, *proseuchomai*, appears in various New Testament passages. It is a compound of the preposition *pros* ("to" or "towards") and *echomail* ("to wish" or "to pray"). The term implies a directional focus in prayer, emphasizing communication with God.[6]

Praying in the Spirit doesn't refer to the specific words we use but our method of prayer. It means praying according to the Spirit's leading, focusing on what the Spirit prompts us to pray for. Romans 8:26 tells us, *"In the same way, the Spirit helps us in our weakness. We do not know what we ought to pray for, but the Spirit himself intercedes for us through wordless groans."*

Some, based on 1 Corinthians 14:15, equate praying in the Spirit with praying in tongues. We read in 1 Corinthians 14:14 that when a person prays in tongues, they don't understand what they're saying, since it's spoken in an unknown language. Moreover, no one else can understand what is being said either—that is, unless there is an interpreter (1 Corinthians 14:27–28).

However, in Ephesians 6:18, Paul instructs us to *"pray in the Spirit on all occasions with all kinds of prayers and requests."* If neither the person praying nor others understand what is being said, how can we pray with all kinds of prayers and requests for all the saints? Therefore, praying in the Spirit should be understood as praying in the power of the Spirit, guided by the Spirit, and according to His will—not necessarily as praying in tongues.

I pray that God will empower me to pray in the Spirit on all occasions, keeping me alert and connected to His strength so I may stand firm in the spiritual battle. I encourage you to pray this over your life as well, because life is indeed a fight. We must know our weapons, wear them faithfully, and use them.

---

[6] William D. Mounce, *Greek for the Rest of Us: The Essential of Biblical Greek* (Grand Rapids, MI: Zondervan Academic, 2013).

Whatever spiritual warfare you may be facing, I urge you to fight on your knees in prayer while always wearing your spiritual armour to stand firm and hold your ground.

10. A life that counts, fulfilling our God-given mission. The tenth prayer essential is to ask God to make my life count, fulfilling the mission for which I was created. I firmly believe that no one and nothing is a mistake. We each have a purpose.

In the biblical narrative, the creation of human beings involves two distinct actions: creating and forming.

Creating. Genesis 1:27 says, *"So God created mankind in his own image, in the image of God he created them; male and female he created them"* (ESV). This verse focuses on the broader concept of creation, highlighting the divine and spiritual aspect of human beings being made in the image of God.

The word mankind is derived from the Old English term *manncynn*, with *mann* referring to a person and *cynn* referring to a kind or race. The term has its roots in Germanic languages, similar to *mennisco* in high German and *mannkyn* in Old Norse. Modern translations of the Bible may use more gender-inclusive language, such as humanity or humankind, to better reflect contemporary understanding and promote gender inclusivity in the interpretation of the biblical text.

The Hebrew word *bara* signifies the divine act of bringing something into existence out of nothing. It emphasizes our spiritual essence, highlighting our unique status as beings made in God's image.

Forming. Genesis 2:7 says that *"then the Lord God formed the man of dust from the ground and breathed into his nostrils the breath of life, and the man became a living creature"* (ESV).

The Hebrew word *yatsar* denotes the shaping or moulding of preexisting material. This emphasizes the physical aspect of human creation, underscoring our earthly composition.

These two actions, creating and forming, reflect the holistic nature of humanity, encompassing both the spiritual and material dimensions. This dual aspect is crucial for understanding our purpose, for it underscores that we have been created both in the image of God and formed from the dust of the earth.

The nuanced use of language suggests a dual process, emphasizing both the physical formation from dust and the spiritual creation in the image of God. Together, these actions signify the complete and unique creation of human beings.

Understanding this duality is crucial. While our physical form begins with conception, our spiritual creation dates back to the dawn of time. This duality is well developed and supported by Reverent Wilfried Zahui, whose ministry has had a significant impact on my life.

I also firmly believe in Ephesians 2:10, which states, *"For we are His workmanship, created in Christ Jesus for good works, which God prepared beforehand that we should walk in them"* (NKJV). This verse clearly teaches that we are not accidents. God created us intentionally for a purpose.

Actually, He speaks directly to our purpose in Jeremiah 29:11: *"For I know the plans I have for you… plans to prosper you and not to harm you, plans to give you hope and a future."* This verse reassures us that God's plans for our lives are filled with hope and purpose.

Our purpose in life is the very meaning of our existence. Romans 8:28 says, *"And we know that in all things God works for the good of those who love him, who have been called according to his purpose."* God is working everything together for our good when we live according to His purpose. Without knowing this, we often suffer, ignorant of our own significance. We may fall prey to the illusion that our lives don't matter and we have no connection or impact on the world around us.

The Bible offers many insights into man's purpose on the earth, living with a mission. Our purpose is the very meaning of our existence. Bringing my purpose to God helps me gain clarity, because as Proverbs 19:21 says *"Many are the plans in a person's heart, but it is the Lord's purpose that prevails."* This reminds us that while we may have our own plans, ultimately God's purpose will stand. I long to know that purpose and fulfill it.

We see examples of people whose lives counted in profound ways. For instance, Moses was called by God to lead the Israelites out of Egypt. His life was marked by a deep sense of purpose. Despite his initial reluctance, he fulfilled his mission, leading God's people to the Promised Land. His life reminds us that we can accomplish great things when we trust in God's plan, even in the face of overwhelming challenges (Exodus 3–4).

Queen Esther's courage in the face of potential death is a testament to living with purpose. She risked her life to save her people, the Jews, from destruction, embracing the purpose for which she had been positioned in the palace. Her story teaches us that we are placed where we are *"for such a time as this"* (Esther 4:14).

The apostle Paul, once a persecutor of Christians, became one of the most influential figures in the early church. His life was transformed by an encounter with Jesus, and he dedicated the rest of his days to spreading the gospel. Paul's life shows how God can repurpose our past for His glory and use us to fulfill His divine mission (Acts 9, 2 Timothy 4:7–8).

I also ask God to help me become the best version of myself. As he appointed me to be the salt of the earth and light of the world, I need help on a continual basis to deliver. I wouldn't want to miss my purpose.

As I reflect on these truths, I pray that I will accomplish the mission for which I have been created. Whatever the size of my impact, I ask that my life be meaningful and fulfilled in the eyes of Lord. I pray for God to help me live a life that counts, one that is aligned with His divine purpose.

How about you? What purpose has God called you to fulfill? Do you find that your life is fulfilled or are you still searching? Go to God in prayers and He will certainly direct your path and give you the clarity and wisdom you need to live a fulfilled life.

Part Three
PRAYERS FOR OTHERS

As I deepened my relationship with God, I was called to extend our prayers beyond ourselves. In this section, I focus on interceding for others—our family, friends, community, and the world.

As the apostle Paul urges us in 1 Timothy 2:1–2: *"I urge, then, first of all, that petitions, prayers, intercession and thanksgiving be made for all people—for kings and all those in authority, that we may live peaceful and quiet lives in all godliness and holiness."*

These prayers reflect the love and concern I hold for those around me, and I hope they will guide you to lift up others in prayer, trusting in God's power to work in their lives.

PRAYER ESSENTIALS FOR OTHERS

1. Praying for all children, entrusting them to God's care. When I begin my prayers for others, I start with my children, lifting them up by name. I see myself as a steward entrusted by God to care for them for a time, until they embark on their own independent journeys.

I pray for their spiritual, emotional, and physical well-being. I ask God to bring godly men and women into their lives; to bless their studies, work, health, and protection; and to prepare them for their future, including their future spouses and families. I seek wisdom and guidance in my role as their mother so I may support them in the way they need.

I also pray for all children I know, whether in my own family or in the community.

Children are a gift from God and hold a special place in His heart. The Bible emphasizes their value and our responsibility to nurture them. Psalm 127:3–4 tells us, *"Children are a heritage from the Lord, offspring a reward from him. Like arrows in the hands of a warrior are children born in one's youth."* This imagery shows us that children are not only a blessing but instruments through which God's purposes can be fulfilled in the world.

In the New Testament, Jesus Himself showed great love and respect for children. In Matthew 19:13–14, we read,

> Then people brought little children to Jesus for him to place his hands on them and pray for them. But the disciples rebuked them.
>
> Jesus said, "Let the little children come to me, and do not hinder them, for the kingdom of heaven belongs to such as these."

This passage highlights Jesus's view of children as precious and worthy of blessing, illustrating their importance in God's kingdom.

Consider the story of Samuel. Hannah, his mother, prayed earnestly for a child, and when God answered her prayer she dedicated Samuel to the Lord's service.

Samuel grew up to be a prophet who played a crucial role in the history of Israel, anointing both Saul and David as kings (1 Samuel 1–3). This example demonstrates how a child raised under God's care and guidance can significantly impact God's work.

Even if you don't have children of your own, you likely know some—whether they're friends' children, nieces, nephews, or children in your community. Praying for children is crucial because they represent the future generation that will shape the world. Proverbs 22:6 advises, *"Start children off on the way they should go, and even when they are old they will not turn from it."* This wisdom emphasizes the importance of instilling godly values in children from a young age, shaping their character and future decisions.

Praying for children's safety and well-being is especially important in a world where many suffer from child labour, abuse, and neglect. The Bible repeatedly calls us to protect and care for the vulnerable, and children are among the most vulnerable in society. Jesus's warning in Matthew 18:6 is stark:

> If anyone causes one of these little ones—those who believe in me—to stumble, it would be better for them to have a large millstone hung around their neck and to be drowned in the depths of the sea.

This verse underscores the gravity of our responsibility to safeguard children.

The future is not as distant as we might think. The children we pray for today are the leaders, decision-makers, and influencers of tomorrow. Their spiritual and emotional health is critical for their development into stable and responsible adults.

Therefore, lifting up children in prayer is an essential act of love and foresight, entrusting them into the hands of the one who loves them most. By praying for them, we contribute to their growth and protection and play a part in shaping a future that honours God. Consider the story of Job, who prayed for his children regularly, asking for God's protection.

It is vital to pray for the safety of children, their protection from child labour and abuse, and for those in the foster care and adoption systems. Jesus Himself highlighted the importance of children in Matthew 19:14: *"Let the little children come to me, and do not hinder them, for the kingdom of heaven belongs to such as these."* This shows how dearly God holds children in His heart and how significant it is for us to pray for them.

We ought to lift children up in prayer. The healthier they are raised, the more emotionally stable they tend to become in their lives tomorrow. Proverbs 20:11 says, *"Even small children are known by their actions, so is their conduct really pure and upright?"* This verse reminds us that children, though young, are observed by others and their actions reflect their upbringing.

In the Bible, we see examples of children who grew to fulfill significant roles in God's plan. Samuel was dedicated to the Lord from a young age and became a great prophet who guided Israel (1 Samuel 1:27–28). Timothy, a young man nurtured in faith by his mother and grandmother, became a close companion of Paul and leader in the early church (2 Timothy 1:5). The children we pray for today will become the best leaders, prophets, and disciples of tomorrow.

I pray that the Lord will continue to work in the lives of the children, guiding, protecting, and helping them to grow in His wisdom and love. May all the children be equipped to face the challenges of the future with faith and courage.

Is there one child in your life who needs prayer?

2. Praying for my spouse. When I pray for my spouse, I lift him up to God, asking for blessings in every area of his life. I pray for his spiritual, physical, and emotional well-being, his relationship with God, our marriage, and his interactions with family and colleagues. I seek God's guidance and favour on his work, purpose in life, and journey of faith.

Praying for a spouse involves covering their entire being—spiritually, physically, and emotionally. I ask God to strengthen my spouse's faith, help him grow closer to Him, and fill him with wisdom and peace. This is crucial for Christian marriage, because spiritual oneness is at the heart of a God-centred union.

I fondly recall attending a marriage conference I attended with my spouse. There, we learned about the marriage pyramid: God is at the top and the husband and wife are at the base. The closer each spouse individually draws to God, the closer they naturally draw to each other. Conversely, the deterioration of a godly marriage often begins when one spouse drifts away from God.

This idea is reinforced in Matthew 6:33: *"But seek first his kingdom and his righteousness, and all these things will be given to you as well."* When both partners prioritize their relationship with God, they cultivate a foundation of respect, love, and unity that strengthens their bond.

Only when both respect the God who sees them in secret can they truly honour and respect each other in public.

C.S. Lewis captures this beautifully: "When I have learned to love God better than my earthly dearest, I shall love my earthly dears better than I do now."[7] This reminds us that loving God above all deepens and enriches our earthly relationships.

In addition to spiritual well-being, I pray for my spouse's physical and financial health, asking for protection, vitality, and provision. I also pray for his emotional well-being, seeking God's comfort, joy, and peace in his life. Through prayer, I entrust every aspect of his being to God's care, knowing that He is faithful to hear and answer.

In 1 Thessalonians 5:23, we read, *"May God himself, the God of peace, sanctify you through and through. May your whole spirit, soul and body be kept blameless at the coming of our Lord Jesus Christ."* We are reminded to pray for our loved ones' complete sanctification and protection. Therefore, I pray for the physical and the spiritual well-being of my spouse.

Philippians 4:6–7 encourages to pray for emotional strength:

> Do not be anxious about anything, but in every situation, by prayer and petition, with thanksgiving, present your requests to God. And the peace of God, which transcends all understanding, will guard your hearts and your minds in Christ Jesus.

This passage reminds us to seek God's peace for emotional stability.

Praying for a spouse's relationship with God is crucial. I ask God to deepen his faith and guide him in his walk with the Lord. Additionally, I pray for harmony and love in his relationships with family members, both immediate and extended.

I pray that God's Word will illuminate his path and guide him in his spiritual journey, as Psalm 119:105 states, *"Your word is a lamp for my feet, a light on my path."*

---

[7] C.S. Lewis, *The Collected Letters of C.S. Lewis, Volume III: Narnia, Cambridge, and Joy*, ed. Walter Hooper (San Francisco, CA: Harper, 2007), 47–48.

Colossians 3:13 advises, *"Bear with each other and forgive one another if any of you has a grievance against someone. Forgive as the Lord forgave you."* This verse highlights the importance of forgiveness and love in our family dynamics.

I pray for success and fulfillment in my spouse's work and that he will find purpose and satisfaction in his career. I ask God to reveal His plans for his life and empower him to achieve his goals.

Even if you don't have a spouse, praying for couples is a powerful way to support and bless others. Couples play a crucial role in our lives and society, and praying for their relationships and challenges is both meaningful and impactful.

Genesis 2:24 states, *"That is why a man leaves his father and mother and is united to his wife, and they become one flesh."* This underscores the importance of prayer for unity and strength in marriages.

The well-known passage in Proverbs 31 provides a model for praying for one's spouse and family. Proverbs 31:10–31 describes a virtuous woman whose prayers and actions bless her husband and family. I seek to embody these virtues in my prayers and in my role as a spouse.

In summary, praying for a spouse includes asking for God's blessings in every facet of life—spiritual, physical, emotional, and relational. Whether you have a spouse or are praying for couples in general, these prayers are vital in supporting and uplifting those we care about.

In praying for my spouse, I pray that God will bless him in all aspects of his life, guide him in his walk with Him, and fulfill his purpose. I pray that he experiences God's favour and protection in all his endeavours. I pray for God to bless the family, strengthening their relationships and helping them reflect God's love and grace in their lives.

If you are looking to be in a relationship, you can start praying for your future partners. Are there any couples you want to pray for on a regular basis?

3. Praying for my family, embracing each member. When I pray for my family, I include each member—my father, brothers, sisters, aunties, uncles, their families, and their kids, including spouses and children as well as cousins, nieces, and nephews. I lift up those who may be experiencing difficult times, seeking God's intervention and blessing for each one.

Praying for family members involves asking for God's blessings and guidance in their lives, both individually and collectively. I pray for their spiritual growth, physical health, emotional stability, and relational harmony.

Colossians 1:9 says, *"We continually ask God to fill you with the knowledge of his will through all the wisdom and understanding that the Spirit gives."* This highlights the importance of seeking God's wisdom and understanding for our loved ones. It is a reminder of our desire for the overall well-being of family members.

When any family member is going through a difficult time, I bring their specific struggles before God, asking for His comfort, strength, and guidance. I pray for resolution, healing, and support during challenging periods.

Psalm 34:18 tells us, *"The Lord is close to the brokenhearted and saves those who are crushed in spirit,"* assuring us of God's presence and healing for those who are hurting. I pray for clarity and direction for family members facing decisions or challenges.

I also pray for healthy, loving relationships within my family. I ask God to foster unity, understanding, and forgiveness among us, and to help us support and uplift each other.

Ephesians 4:2–3 states, *"Be completely humble and gentle; be patient, bearing with one another in love. Make every effort to keep the unity of the Spirit through the bond of peace."* This verse guides us in maintaining harmonious relationships.

Recall Colossians 3:13, which underscores the importance of forgiveness in family dynamics.

Speaking of forgiveness, have you felt that it's so much difficult to forgive the ones who are closest to us than the ones who are far away? Maybe this is because we're so used to them or see them more often. But we have to choose to forgive over and over.

In addition to the immediate family, I lift up extended family members, such as cousins and their families, asking for God's blessings and support in their lives.

As 1 Timothy 5:8 says, *"Anyone who does not provide for their relatives, and especially for their own household, has denied the faith and is worse than an unbeliever."* This emphasizes the importance of caring for and praying for all family members.

When I bring my family in prayer before my Lord, I ask him for His blessings upon each member. I pray for their spiritual growth, physical health, emotional stability, and harmonious relationships. For those who are experiencing difficult times, I seek His comfort, guidance, and healing. I ask Him to help us to support one another and reflect His love in our family interactions and that His presence be felt in every aspect of our lives, so we may grow together in faith and unity.

How about you? Do you need help in your family relationship? Bring your family members up to the altar in prayers.

4. The church family, lifting up the saints and shepherds. I also pray for believers, pastors, my church family, and the advancement of God's kingdom on earth.

As a leader in the women's ministry, I understand the profound impact of prayer on our community and beyond. My prayer life extends to the believers I serve, including my pastor, the women and their families, and all those involved in ministry. The Bible teaches us to pray for all saints, and I take this to heart.

In my prayers, I lift up fellow believers, asking God to strengthen their faith, guide their steps, and provide for their needs. Ephesians 6:18 instructs us to *"pray in the Spirit on all occasions with all kinds of prayers and requests,"* reminding us to be vigilant and persistent in our prayers for others. I pray for their spiritual growth, protection from temptation, and encouragement in their walk with Christ.

I also pray for my pastor, whose leadership is crucial to our spiritual community. I ask God to bless him with wisdom, strength, and clarity as he shepherds us. We read in 1 Thessalonians 5:12–13 an encouragement for us to *"acknowledge those who work hard among you, who care for you in the Lord and who admonish you. Hold them in the highest regard in love because of their work"* (NKJV). This reflects the importance of supporting our spiritual leaders through prayer.

As part of leading the women's ministry, I prioritize praying for the women involved, their families, and their unique needs. Proverbs 31:26 describes the virtuous woman as someone who *"opens her mouth with wisdom, and on her tongue is the law of kindness"* (NKJV). I ask God to empower these women with wisdom, strength, and grace in their roles as wives, mothers, and leaders.

Prayer meetings and Bible studies are vital for spiritual growth and community. I pray for these gatherings to be filled with the Holy Spirit's guidance, that they may foster deep connections with God and one another.

Colossians 3:16 encourages us, *"Let the message of Christ dwell among you richly as you teach and admonish one another with all wisdom…"* I seek God's blessing on these meetings, that they may bear fruit in our lives and strengthen our faith.

Our church is involved in various ministries and supports missionaries around the world. I pray for all these ministries—such as the children, youth, young adult, elders, widows, orphans, ushers, etc.—to thrive and for the missionaries to be protected and effective in their work. We are reminded in 2 Corinthians 1:11 to help each other in prayer, *"that thanks may be given by many persons on our behalf for the gift granted to us through many"* (NKJV). I ask God to use these efforts to spread His love and truth globally.

I have a prayer group in which anyone can share a prayer request and one of us will spontaneously pray, even it's an unspoken prayer. In my women's ministry, we have a prayer partner program in which women come in a group of two or three, maximum, to pray regularly for one another. We have received great testimonies about the blessings that have come from this. We also have a prayer box at church for anonymous prayer requests, and these are shared with a small group.

This is why I am a strong supporter of EMCI TV and a proud member of their partnership network. EMCI places an extraordinary emphasis on prayer, making it a cornerstone of their ministry. Every week, the EMCI team fervently prays for their partners and their extended families, known as *la famille des partenaires*. This heartfelt commitment reflects their deep belief in the power of intercession.

Additionally, Dr. Moussa Touré and his 24/7 intercessory network Watchmen faithfully intercede on behalf of all who support EMCI. Their prayers cover every area of life—health, soul, family, relationships, and finances. They remind God of His promises to those who seek first His Kingdom, as stated in Matthew 6:33: *"But seek first his kingdom and his righteousness, and all these things will be given to you as well."* They also draw encouragement from Hebrews 6:10: *"God is not unjust; he will not forget your work and the love you have shown him as you have helped his people and continue to help them."*

The team not only prays for general prosperity but also gives thanks to God for the generosity of their partners, whose contributions allow them to preach the good news to all creation through various media platforms.

For those with specific needs, EMCI invites them to share their prayer topics. These requests are printed and added to their prayer walls, serving as powerful points of contact with faith.

Isn't this remarkable? I have witnessed firsthand how EMCI's ministry has flourished year after year, evidence of their unwavering commitment to the Lord's work and their reliance on the transformative power of prayer. Through their example, I am reminded of the truth in James 5:16: *"The prayer of a righteous person is powerful and effective."*

Finally, I pray for the advancement of God's kingdom on the earth. Matthew 6:10 asks us to pray that *"your kingdom come, your will be done, on earth as it is in heaven."* I pray for God's will to be done in our lives and in our communities around the globe. I also pray for His kingdom to grow as more people come to know Him and experience His grace.

These prayers aren't just an obligation but a privilege. By lifting these requests to God, we partner with Him in His work and contribute to the growth and strengthening of His church. I pray that our efforts will bring glory to God and further His kingdom, both locally and globally.

In summary, I pray for the Lord's continued blessing on all those I lift up in prayer, to guide, protect, and empower them to fulfill His will. I pray that my Lord's kingdom will come and His will be done on earth as it is in heaven.

How about you? Can you think of any believers or community that you feel need your constant prayers?

5. Workplace blessings, praying for my career and colleagues. In my prayer journey, I dedicate time to pray for my workplace, understanding that its success directly impacts my own. I lift up my boss, colleagues, and supervisors, asking God to bless them with wisdom, guidance, and protection. I also pray for the success of company projects, knowing that when the company thrives it is a reflection of our collective efforts.

I ask God to grant my boss wisdom and understanding in his leadership role. Proverbs 16:9 says, *"In their hearts humans plan their course, but the Lord establishes their steps."* I pray that God will direct my boss's decisions and bless his family, providing him with strength and support.

For my colleagues and supervisors, I pray for harmonious working relationships and for God's guidance in our interactions. Ecclesiastes 4:9 reminds us, *"Two are better than one, because they have a good return for their labor..."* I seek God's favour on our teamwork and cooperation.

I pray for the success of company projects and for God to bless our efforts with innovation and effectiveness. Proverbs 21:5 states, *"The plans of the diligent lead to profit as surely as haste leads to poverty."* I ask for God's guidance to make prudent and effective decisions that contribute to the success of our projects.

Protection and wisdom in the workplace are crucial. Psalm 121:7–8 assures us, *"The Lord will keep you from all harm—he will watch over your life; the Lord will watch over your coming and going both now and forevermore."* I pray for God's protection over everyone in the workplace and for His guidance in all our endeavours.

I seek God's blessing for intelligence and creative ideas so I can excel in my work. James 1:5 says, *"If any of you lacks wisdom, you should ask God, who gives generously to all without finding fault, and it will be given to you."* I ask for God's wisdom to apply innovative solutions and contribute meaningfully to the company.

For readers who don't currently have a job, I pray for future employment opportunities. Matthew 7:7 promises, *"Ask and it will be given to you; seek and you will find; knock and the door will be opened to you."* I ask God to provide them with suitable job opportunities and to prepare them for future roles.

I also pray for entrepreneurs who take risks to create job opportunities for others. Proverbs 22:29 notes, *"Do you see someone skilled in their work? They will serve before kings; they will not serve before officials of low rank."* I pray that God will bless their endeavours and reward their hard work and dedication.

The story of Joseph in Genesis 39–41 is a powerful example of how God can bless and elevate someone in their workplace. Despite facing trials, Joseph's faithfulness and diligence led him to rise to a position of great influence in Egypt. His story illustrates how God can work through our professional lives to achieve His purposes and bring about success.

Praying for the workplace helps us recognize the interconnectedness of our work and our faith. By seeking God's guidance, wisdom, and protection for ourselves and others in the workplace, we contribute to creating a positive and productive environment where God's presence and blessings are evident.

Have you ever prayed for your work? Have you taken your work for granted and found that this isn't necessary? I am confident that it is a much needed area for prayer.

6. Friendship prayers, standing in the gap for my friends. I keep dedicated notes about the friends I pray for, lifting them up to God. I also keep a journal with my friends' names with a word about them to lift them in prayers. Whether they're going through specific challenges or have requested prayer, I focus on interceding for them, asking God to bless and guide them in every aspect of their lives.

When friends reach out with specific prayer requests, or if I know they're facing difficulties, I dedicate time to pray for their needs. James 5:16 says, *"The prayer of a righteous person is powerful and effective."* I believe that through prayer we can support our friends in their times of need and trust in God's power to bring about positive change.

Friendship is a precious gift, and I pray that God will bless this gift in my life and in the lives of my friends. Proverbs 27:9 says, *"Perfume and incense bring joy to the heart, and the pleasantness of a friend springs from their heartfelt advice."* I ask God to enhance the joy and

PART THREE: PRAYERS FOR OTHERS

encouragement that come from true friendship and foster deeper, more meaningful connections.

I pray for my friends' overall well-being—spiritual, emotional, and physical. I ask God to grant them strength, peace, and health. 3 John 1:2 states, *"Dear friend, I pray that you may enjoy good health and that all may go well with you, even as your soul is getting along well."* This verse reminds me to pray for my friends' holistic well-being, trusting that God cares about every aspect of their lives. I pray for God's wisdom and guidance in their lives, asking Him to help them make sound decisions and navigate their challenges.

I pray for God's protection over my friends and for His comfort in their times of sorrow or distress. Psalm 91:1–2 assures us, *"Whoever dwells in the shelter of the Most High will rest in the shadow of the Almighty. I will say of the Lord, 'He is my refuge and my fortress, my God, in whom I trust.'"* I ask God to be their refuge and fortress, providing safety and peace.

I pray for my friends' spiritual growth and for God's blessings to be evident in their lives. Philippians 1:6 promises *"that he who began a good work in you will carry it on to completion until the day of Christ Jesus."* I trust that God is at work in their lives and will continue to guide and bless them as they grow in their faith.

The story of Job's friends is a poignant example of standing in the gap for one's friends. Job's friends, though initially coming to comfort him, later faced correction for not speaking accurately about God's ways. This story illustrates the importance of genuine, accurate prayer and support for friends in times of trial (Job 42:7–10).

Another example is the friendship of David and Jonathan. Their bond is a testament to the depth of true friendship and mutual support. We read in 1 Samuel 18:1, *"After David had finished talking with Saul, Jonathan became one in spirit with David, and he loved him as himself."* This relationship highlights the power of supporting one another through prayer and encouragement.

For friends who do not yet know Christ, I pray for their hearts to be open to the gospel and for God to use me as a witness. Paul wrote, *"As for other matters, brothers and sisters, pray for us that the message of the*

Lord may spread rapidly and be honored, just as it was with you" (2 Thessalonians 3:1). I pray for opportunities to share my faith and for their eventual acceptance of Christ.

By standing in the gap through prayer, I contribute to the well-being of my friends and support them in their journeys. I trust that God values these prayers and will work in their lives according to His will.

How about you? Do you take the time to pray for your friends? I encourage you to stand in the gap for them.

7. Healing prayers, petitioning for the sick. In my prayer life, I dedicate a portion of my time to interceding for those who are ill or in need of healing. I keep a list of prayer requests for sickness, remembering both those who have shared their needs with me and those who may not be aware of my prayers.

This is the time to ask my perfect heavenly Father, who is a great healer, to powerfully heal me in a holistic way physically, emotionally, mentally, and spiritually, because this is the will of my God for me. As 3 John 1:2 says, *"Beloved, I pray that you may prosper in all things and be health, even as your soul prospers"* (NKJV).

Years ago, I started praying over myself before consulting a doctor because I believe that my God is the greatest doctor by excellence.

I maintain a list of individuals who need healing, both in my circle and beyond. I pray for their physical restoration, emotional comfort, and spiritual strength. James 5:14–15 instructs us,

> Is anyone among you sick? Let them call the elders of the church to pray over them and anoint them with oil in the name of the Lord. And the prayer offered in faith will make the sick person well; the Lord will raise them up. If they have sinned, they will be forgiven.

This verse assures us of the power of prayer in bringing about healing.

Sometimes I come across situations where people are in distress, such as seeing an ambulance or hearing of a crisis. In these moments, I take the opportunity to lift these strangers up in prayer, even if I don't know them. This is because 1 Thessalonians 5:17 encourages us to *"pray continually,"* which includes spontaneous prayers for those in need.

When friends or family members are ill, I lift them up before God, asking for His healing touch and comforting presence. Psalm 30:2 says, *"Lord my God, I called to you for help, and you healed me."* I ask God to grant them physical healing, peace, and the strength to endure their trials.

When I was young and in the middle of studying for my bachelor's degree, I had a close friend who stayed late after class with me to finish an assignment. On his way home, he was shot and gravely wounded. Upon receiving the news, I was devastated. I spent the night on my knees, crying and praying for him.

In the morning, I learned that the surgery was successful and his life had been spared. I was certain that God had performed a miracle.

I later visited this friend and was so happy to see him alive. I never told him that I had prayed for him all night, but I was confident that God had answered my prayers.

I also recall the fear of losing one of my daughters when she was two years old. She was hospitalized repeatedly for a respiratory virus but seemed to be getting better.

After an international trip, however, her respiratory problems returned. She was struggling to breathe. My two greatest fears were that we didn't have health insurance and we wouldn't be covered for medical expenses.

I cried out to God, saying, "Oh Lord, You have already entrusted her to me. I am going to be a good steward. Please don't take her away from me, please…"

That night, I purchased a ticket to take her back to her birth country. Upon arrival, we went directly to the hospital, where she was taken in immediately. She spent the week in hospital and she was placed on oxygen. The doctors told us that we had made it there just in time.

I cried and prayed for a complete and final healing, but the doctors told me she would need medication for the rest of her life and might never be the same again.

Today she is the healthiest and happiest child I know. She has never taken medication or been sick since then, and I believe this was due to God's intervention. He heard my cry and miraculously restored her hundred percent. James 5:15 was manifested in my life: *"And the prayer of faith will save the one who is sick, and the Lord will raise him up. And if he has committed sins, he will be forgiven"* (ESV).

When someone shares their healing testimony, I give thanks to God for His work in their lives. Psalm 107:19–20 states, *"Then they cried to the Lord in their trouble, and he saved them from their distress. He sent out his word and healed them; he rescued them from the grave."*

I acknowledge and celebrate God's miraculous work in the healing of others. I also express gratitude when healing occurs and people share their testimonies of recovery. I write them down as a reminder for those times when I feel discouraged and my faith wavers. The help me remember that my God is the same yesterday, today, and tomorrow; He never changes and I must stay attached to Him, just as branches are attached to the tree.

Healing isn't only physical but also emotional and spiritual. I pray for holistic recovery for those who are suffering, asking God to mend broken hearts and renew spirits. Psalm 147:3 promises, *"He heals the brokenhearted and binds up their wounds."* I seek God's comfort and restoration for those who are struggling emotionally or spiritually.

The story of Job's healing is a profound example of recovery after intense suffering. After enduring great loss and illness, Job was restored and blessed by God. Job 42:10 says, *"After Job had prayed for his friends, the Lord restored his fortunes and gave him twice as much as he had before."* This story illustrates the power of prayer and faith in the face of suffering.

Another example is the healing of the blind man in John 9:1–7. Jesus healed him by bringing back his sight through His saliva and telling him to wash in the pool of Siloam. This miracle not only restored the man's sight but also demonstrated Jesus's compassion and divine authority. The man's healing led to a testimony of God's power and glory.

In addition to personal prayers, I also pray for the broader context of healing. I pray for those who are working to bring healing and comfort to others, such as medical professionals, social workers, first responders, caregivers, and systems that support the people who are not only sick physically but also spiritually, emotionally, and mentally. For those who may face health challenges in the future or are preparing for medical procedures, I pray in advance for their comfort, wisdom, and healing. I trust that God is aware of their needs and will respond according to His will.

By dedicating time to healing prayers, I trust in God's power to bring restoration and peace to those who are sick. I believe that through these prayers I am participating in God's work of healing and offering support and hope to those in need.

How about you? I encourage you to pray for the sick to the Great Healer, because Jesus is the doctor who brings great healing to all who are sick.

8. Prayers of forgiveness. Forgiveness is the cornerstone of healing and spiritual growth. When I pray for those who have hurt me, I ask God to help me release any lingering bitterness or resentment in my heart.

This is when I sit down and reflect on the events of my troubled life as if I were examining someone else's story, carefully guarding against self-justification and looking at the facts honestly. I consider what I've said or done in haste, out of anger or desperation, that have made my situation worse and reflect on how I can learn from them. I then resolve not to repeat past mistakes and ask God to help me identify triggers as a reminder to pause and think before I act or speak when tempted or pressured into irrational behaviour. I seek His help in removing these impulses and growing into the person He wants me to become.

Forgiving others isn't just about freeing them from their wrongs but also liberating myself from the chains of unforgiveness. Ephesians 4:31–32 advises, *"Get rid of all bitterness, rage and anger, brawling and slander, along with every form of malice. Be kind and compassionate to one another, forgiving each other, just as in Christ God forgave you."* Through prayer, I strive to align my heart with Christ's example of forgiveness and grace.

A few years ago, I began writing the names of those who hurt me in my prayer notebook, along with their offences, to pray for them. This practice has helped me release them from my heart and discover patterns in the reasons I feel hurt. My top three triggers are abuse, deceit, and rejection. Recognizing these triggers has led me to question why they affect me so deeply and whether I need healing in these areas. For example, abuse in any form is terrifying and may require therapy to deal with the underlying pain to prevent repeating the cycle.

Have you ever noticed the same issues resurfacing in your life? Why does the same lesson seem to repeat itself? It might be time to step back, learn the lesson, and move forward rather than remaining stuck in the same pattern.

It took me decades to understand why I kept experiencing rejection, which made it difficult for me to form lasting relationships. Facing this issue with courage, I realized that it stemmed from my childhood. When I was not yet three years old, during a period of great turmoil in my country, my school was dismissed early. I waited outside for my parents to pick me up, but no one came.

Since my mom usually took the same road to bring me to school, I mustered the courage to walk home by myself, despite being really scared. My country's turmoil meant there were often shootings and burning tires. I remember people pulling me out of the way so cars wouldn't run over me; the drivers had difficulty seeing me because I was so small.

When I finally got home, my mom was very upset to hear that I had walked alone. My dad was proud of me. But neither of them understood why I had come home early. They later realized that they had forgotten about the school's early dismissal.

Although I eventually discovered the reason for me having been forgotten at school that day, I still remember the fear of abandonment I faced.

Fast-forward to when I was seven years old. My father, whom I adored, left my mother and me to marry another woman. His absence created in me a deep-seated fear of abandonment, leading me to avoid attachment to others or to expect rejection, even from those who seemed loving. This realization, brought to light through prayer and meditation, has allowed me to absolve those who have hurt me, forgive my father, and work on healing in this area of my life.

When we are hurt, delving deep into the reasons for it can resolve the root issues, enabling us to better understand those who hurt us and forgive them. But for that to happen we need to be willing to be transparent and vulnerable with ourselves and the Lord.

Forgiveness also involves forgiving yourself. Have you ever been angry with yourself for things you did or didn't do? I have. We can be so tough on ourselves.

During my journey, I reached a point where I couldn't forgive myself until I heard my perfect heavenly Father say, "If I, who am perfect, forgive you, how dare you not forgive yourself and move on?" It takes time, but I've started to work on it. Healing is possible.

It will be difficult to forgive others when we don't forgive ourselves. Remember, everything starts from within. I'm not suggesting that we have a careless attitude or sugarcoat our actions, but punishing ourselves forever isn't a healthy way to live.

I used to say, "Yeah, I forgive, but I don't forget." However, God's Word teaches us that not only does He forgive, but He also chooses to forget. Hebrews 8:12 says, *"For I will forgive their wickedness and will remember their sins no more."* This truth is reinforced in Isaiah 43:25: *"I, even I, am he who blots out your transgressions, for my own sake, and remembers your sins no more."* It's crucial to make every effort to forget past wrongs so they don't haunt our sleep. Holding onto offences is like carrying bags of trash with us through life. No one needs that.

When praying about forgiveness, it's important to reflect on the ways in which we may have hurt others—through our words, actions, or thoughts. I ask God for forgiveness for these offences and seek His guidance in making amends and breaking these patterns. As Matthew 5:23–24 instructs,

> Therefore, if you are offering your gift at the altar and there remember that your brother or sister has something against you, leave your gift there in front of the altar. First go and be reconciled to them; then come and offer your gift.

This passage highlights the importance of reconciliation and repairing relationships wherever possible.

I also use Galatians 5:19–21 to examine my life and identify any sinful behaviours or attitudes I might be struggling with: *"The acts of the flesh are obvious: sexual immorality, impurity and debauchery; idolatry and witchcraft; hatred, discord, jealousy, fits of rage, selfish ambition, dissensions, factions and envy; drunkenness, orgies, and the like."* Who among us can claim innocence on all these counts?

This inventory helps me to recognize the areas where I need to seek God's forgiveness and transformation. Just as I pray for the fruit of the Spirit to manifest in my life, I must also guard against the enemy sowing weeds among the good seeds. It's vital to ensure these weeds of the flesh don't take root. As the saying goes, while we may not be able to stop the birds from flying over our heads, we can prevent them from making a nest.

Anger is one area of weakness I struggle with. While anger itself isn't a sin, it can lead to sin, as we read in Ephesians 4:26: *"In your anger do not sin: do not let the sun go down while you are still angry…"* My challenge lies in resolving anger before it festers.

My spouse, on the other hand, is slow to anger, which sometimes frustrates me, as I misinterpret his calmness as indifference.

Yet I realize that just as we all have areas of weakness, we also have strengths. It's important to acknowledge our weaknesses, work on them, and be grateful for our strengths.

As part of my forgiveness prayers, I perform a fearless moral inventory of myself. This process involves undertaking a thorough and honest examination of my actions, thoughts, and motivations. I ask God for help in identifying areas where I need to repent and seek His strength to overcome these struggles. This inventory is akin to the fourth step in the twelve-step program. It is an opportunity for self-reflection and spiritual growth. In doing so, by removing the plank in my own eye first, it has helped me address Matthew 7:3–5:

> Why do you look at the speck of sawdust in your brother's eye and pay no attention to the plank in your

own eye? How can you say to your brother, "Let me take the speck out of your eye," when all the time there is a plank in your own eye? You hypocrite, first take the plank out of your own eye, and then you will see clearly to remove the speck from your brother's eye.

For example, it's crucial to continually ask my heavenly Father to help me manage my overthinking because ignoring my weaknesses doesn't make them disappear. They often grow as we do.

My anger once led me to commit a regrettable act, teaching me a profound lesson about not playing God in people's lives but learning to let go and let God. If you need to bring to the Lord any acts of the flesh for healing, I encourage you to do so. Doing so will bring you to a place of asking for forgiveness, and forgiving yourself as well, so you can learn from this shortcoming and move forward with less baggage.

Additionally, 1 John 2:16–17 reminds us,

> For everything in the world—the lust of the flesh, the lust of the eyes, and the pride of life—comes not from the Father but from the world. The world and its desires pass away, but whoever does the will of God lives forever.

Reflecting on these verses helps me identify worldly desires that may be influencing my behaviour and seek to align my actions with God's will.

For example, I love sweets. I find them hard to resist even though I know they aren't good for me. This can indeed be considered a form of lust, which includes any strong desires or cravings for physical pleasure or gratification that may go against what's beneficial for me. Lust isn't always something extreme; it can be something very small that you don't realize takes up so much space in your life. It can be your phone, social media, or something else you feel so attached to that you feel lack when you're not engaging with it. That's when it becomes dangerous. A healthy life is about balance in everything.

A way to guard against this is to refrain from watching certain shows or movies because they tempt you away from what's spiritually uplifting. Failing to guard against this can lead to envy, greed, and other harmful thoughts.

Constantly pursuing diplomas and knowledge, especially if it's driven by a desire to boost one's status, reputation, or self-worth, can be an example of the pride of life. Seeking knowledge isn't wrong, but if the motivation is rooted in pride or a desire to elevate ourselves above others, it becomes problematic.

On the other hand, if the motivation is simply to acquire more knowledge to improve one's life and the lives of others, it is a noble pursuit.

I bring all these areas to God in prayer, surrendering them and asking for His guidance to better align my desires with His will. Recognizing these weaknesses allows me to ask for His strength to resist temptation and grow in righteousness. I often remind myself of the words in James 1:14–15: *"but each person is tempted when they are dragged away by their own evil desire and enticed. Then, after desire has conceived, it gives birth to sin; and sin, when it is full-grown, gives birth to death."* This passage serves as a powerful reminder that unchecked desires can lead to sin, which ultimately leads to spiritual death.

In this journey of forgiveness, I seek to replace sinful behaviours with actions that reflect the fruit of the Spirit, as described in Galatians 5:22–23: *"But the fruit of the Spirit is love, joy, peace, forbearance, kindness, goodness, faithfulness, gentleness and self-control. Against such things there is no law."* I ask God to cultivate these qualities in me so my actions may glorify Him. Our human nature needs something to replace the void. Therefore, it's not about just stopping certain behaviours, but about finding healthy and balanced ways to replace them.

Finally, in this process of forgiveness, it's essential to remember that it's not a one-time event but an ongoing journey. There will be times when memories of past hurt resurface, producing temptations to hold onto resentment. In those moments, we remind ourselves of Colossians 3:13: *"Bear with each other and forgive one another if any of you has a grievance against someone. Forgive as the Lord forgave you."* This helps me renew my commitment to forgiveness, knowing that God has forgiven me countless times.

I also speak specific prayers for my enemies, both known and unknown. This helps me stay vigilant in the face of potential spiritual attacks.

It's vital to pray, but we must also be mindful of what Scripture teaches us about being alert, for the Word of God makes it clear that we are called to watch and pray. Have you ever noticed that the Bible instructs us to be watchful before we pray? In *Luke 21:36*, Jesus says, *"Be always on the watch, and pray that you may be able to escape all that is about to happen, and that you may be able to stand before the Son of Man."* This reminds us that while prayer is essential, we must also remain spiritually vigilant, discerning the dangers around us.

Too often we pray without maintaining the necessary vigilance. Prayer doesn't mean we act carelessly, like crossing the road on a red light simply because we have prayed for safety. That would be irresponsible. God's Word teaches us to act wisely and be alert to the realities of life. In *1 Peter 5:8* we are told, *"Be alert and of sober mind. Your enemy the devil prowls around like a roaring lion looking for someone to devour."* This highlights the importance of remaining watchful and sober-minded because the enemy is always seeking opportunities to attack.

> *Too often we pray without maintaining the necessary vigilance. Prayer doesn't mean we act carelessly, like crossing the road on a red light simply because we have prayed for safety.*

Therefore, I continually pray for God's protection over the schemes of the enemy. I ask the Lord to cover me with the blood of Jesus, to help me remain vigilant and keep my mind clear and focused.

As believers, we are in a spiritual battlefield, not a playground. This is why we must put on the full armour of God, as described in *Ephesians 6:11*, to stand firm against the enemy's plans.

With God's help, I trust that any plot against me will be turned for my good. And if God allows challenges to come my way, I know

He will provide me with the strength to fight and ultimately win the battle.

I encourage you to pray daily for God's protection to equip you with the tools to fight life's everyday battles with a victorious mindset, knowing that we are more than conquerors through Christ who strengthens us.

I also encourage you to reflect on the people you need to forgive, including yourself, and to bring those burdens before God in prayer. Let Him guide you through the process of healing and reconciliation. Forgiveness isn't just about setting others free; it's about setting yourself free from the heavy weight of bitterness and unforgiveness. It's about allowing God to transform your heart and fill it with His peace, love, and joy.

As we embark on this journey, may we find the strength and grace to forgive, and may God's love and peace be our constant companions. Remember, forgiveness is a powerful act of obedience to God, and through it we can experience the fullness of His blessings in our lives.

9. Praying for projects and plans, seeking God's guidance and direction. In prayer essential, I dedicate all my problems, shortcomings, projects, plans, and activities to God. I recognize that while I may have ideas and ambitions, it's crucial to seek God's guidance and align my efforts with His will. As Proverbs 16:3 advises, *"Commit to the Lord whatever you do, and he will establish your plans."* By committing my plans to God, I acknowledge His sovereignty and trust in His wisdom to guide me in the right direction.

Instead of pursuing my plans independently and later asking for God's blessing, I seek spiritual insight to understand His plan for me from the outset. I ask for the discernment to know His will and the strength to follow it. James 1:5 encourages us, *"If any of you lacks wisdom, you should ask God, who gives generously to all without finding fault, and it will be given to you."* This reassures me that God is willing to provide wisdom and direction when I earnestly seek it.

I present my specific projects and plans to God, whether they are short-term tasks or long-term goals. I ask Him to guide me in every detail, ensuring that my actions are aligned with His purposes. Whether it's a new business venture, a personal goal, or a ministry project, I pray for His direction and blessing. Psalm 37:5 says, *"Commit your way to the Lord; trust in him and he will do this..."* This reinforces my commitment to entrust my plans to God, trusting that He will direct my steps.

I pray for the humility to surrender my own plans and desires, seeking instead to follow God's will. I acknowledge that His knowledge and wisdom far surpass my own. As Isaiah 55:8–9 reminds us,

> "For my thoughts are not your thoughts, neither are your ways my ways," declares the Lord. "As the heavens are higher than the earth, so are my ways higher than your ways and my thoughts than your thoughts."

This passage helps me recognize that God's plans are perfect, even when they differ from my own expectations.

As I move forward with my projects, I seek God's guidance in making decisions and navigating challenges. I ask Him to help me discern His will in every aspect and provide clarity and direction, trusting His guidance over my own understanding.

The story of Nehemiah is a powerful example of seeking God's guidance for a project. Nehemiah prayed fervently for the restoration of Jerusalem's walls and sought God's direction throughout the process. Nehemiah 2:4–5 records this prayer:

> The king said to me, "What is it you want?"
> Then I prayed to the God of heaven, and I answered the king, "If it pleases the king and if your servant has found favor in his sight, let him send me to the city in Judah where my ancestors are buried so that I can rebuild it."

Nehemiah's reliance on prayer and God's guidance led to the successful completion of the project.

Another example is Paul's missionary journeys. The apostle constantly sought God's direction for where to go and what to do. Acts

16:6–7 describes how Paul and his companions were guided by the Holy Spirit:

> Paul and his companions traveled throughout the region of Phrygia and Galatia, having been kept by the Holy Spirit from preaching the word in the province of Asia. When they came to the border of Mysia, they tried to enter Bithynia, but the Spirit of Jesus would not allow them to.

Paul's willingness to follow God's lead despite his own plans highlights the importance of seeking divine direction in our endeavours.

As I wait for God's guidance, I pray for patience and faith. I trust that His timing is perfect and that He will reveal His plan in due course. Lamentations 3:25 assures us, *"The Lord is good to those whose hope is in him, to the one who seeks him."* This encourages me to maintain hope and trust in God's goodness as I seek His direction. By dedicating my projects and plans to God and seeking His guidance from the beginning, I aim to align my efforts with His will and trust in His wisdom to lead me in the right direction.

Another area of prayer for me is addressing my dreams and nightmares. Have you ever had dreams that feel so real, so terrifying, that they left you yearning to understand their meaning? Or perhaps you've experienced recurring dreams for years. I have. Like me, you have no peace in sleeping through the nights, going from one nightmare to another, only to wake up exhausted as if you never slept.

This is not what our heavenly Father wants for us. **Proverbs 3:24** says: *"When you lie down, you will not be afraid; when you lie down, your sleep will be sweet."* It is God's will that our sleep be sweet.

If, like me, you have been tormented in your dreams, it may be a sign of spiritual warfare, meaning that it's vital to surrender these experiences to God in prayer. Additionally, exploring deep-seated traumas that might trigger such nightmares is an important step toward healing.

One spiritual leader who has profoundly helped me in the area of dream interpretation is Stephanie Ike Okafor. Her insights and ministry have been a blessing in my journey. I encourage you to explore her teachings if this resonates with you.

During moments of meditation and prayer, I began the practice of writing down my nightmares to identify patterns and gain better understanding. This simple act of reflection has helped me connect the dots and uncover underlying issues.

Alongside these spiritual efforts, seeking the guidance of a trauma therapist can be transformative. Dr. Anita Phillips, a leading Christian trauma therapist, has provided me with a perspective on deep-rooted traumas that has been both enlightening and healing.

Remember, God desires peace for His children—even in their sleep. Jesus Himself assures us in John 14:27, *"Peace I leave with you; my peace I give you. I do not give to you as the world gives. Do not let your hearts be troubled and do not be afraid."* Rest and peace are part of the abundant life He has promised.

If you are struggling with nightmares, I encourage you to seek healing, knowing that God's peace surpasses all understanding and extends to every area of your life, including your dreams.

> *If you are struggling with nightmares, I encourage you to seek healing, knowing that God's peace surpasses all understanding and extends to every area of your life, including your dreams.*

In closeness to my heavenly Father, I even pray about how I would like to die and what I want that transition to be like. This might be surprising, but don't many of us purchase life insurance? Why do we do that? We pay in advance for the benefits our loved ones will receive after we're gone, acknowledging that the time will come when we must transition from this life.

My grand-auntie Ciane just passed away at the age of ninety-eight. We had been hoping to celebrate her one hundredth birthday. Even for those on their deathbed, doctors cannot predict the exact moment of transition. Therefore, why not plan for it and talk to the one who holds control over life and death about how we would like that transition to happen? While He may not reveal the exact time, He did so in the story of Hezekiah in 2 Kings 20:1–6:

> In those days Hezekiah became ill and was at the point of death. The prophet Isaiah son of Amoz went to him and said, "This is what the Lord says: Put your house in order, because you are going to die; you will not recover."
>
> Hezekiah turned his face to the wall and prayed to the Lord, "Remember, Lord, how I have walked before you faithfully and with wholehearted devotion and have done what is good in your eyes." And Hezekiah wept bitterly.
>
> Before Isaiah had left the middle court, the word of the Lord came to him: "Go back and tell Hezekiah, the ruler of my people, 'This is what the Lord, the God of your father David, says: I have heard your prayer and seen your tears; I will heal you. On the third day from now you will go up to the temple of the Lord. I will add fifteen years to your life.'"

This passage shows us that nothing is too great for God. In every stage of life, I bring everything to Him.

How about you? Which prayer item would you be willing to bring into your prayer time? Something about your purpose, your vision, or some issue you are personally dealing with?

Give everything to Him. It will never be too big or too much for Him to handle, and you can be sure that He will provide beyond measure. Your duty is to ask boldly, ask big, and wait confidently and expectantly.

10. Global intercession, praying for my country and the world. My last prayer essential involving global intercession. I dedicate special prayers for my country and the world, focusing on the governments and those in positions of power who make decisions impacting our lives. The

Bible instructs us to pray for our leaders and authorities, recognizing their role in maintaining order and justice.

This is emphasized in 1 Timothy 2:1–2: *"I urge, then, first of all, that petitions, prayers, intercession and thanksgiving be made for all people—for kings and all those in authority, that we may live peaceful and quiet lives in all godliness and holiness."* This reminds me of the importance of praying for those who govern, as their decisions affect the well-being of society.

I pray for our leaders' wisdom and discernment, asking God to guide their decisions and actions. Proverbs 2:6 states, *"For the Lord gives wisdom; from his mouth come knowledge and understanding."* I seek God's intervention to grant leaders the wisdom needed to make just and righteous decisions that align with His will.

I lift up prayers for peace and justice in my country and around the world. The Bible calls us to seek peace and work towards justice. Psalm 33:5 declares, *"The Lord loves righteousness and justice; the earth is full of his unfailing love."* I pray for God's justice to prevail and for efforts to promote peace and reconciliation among nations and communities.

I also intercede for global issues, such as poverty, conflict, and environmental concerns. Matthew 5:14 reminds us of our role in addressing these challenges: *"You are the light of the world. A town built on a hill cannot be hidden."* By praying for help in the face of global challenges, I ask God to inspire and empower individuals and organizations working to address these issues and to bring about positive change.

I specifically pray for the welfare of my own country, including its leaders, economy, and social issues. Jeremiah 29:7 instructs, *"Also, seek the peace and prosperity of the city to which I have carried you into exile. Pray to the Lord for it, because if it prospers, you too will prosper."* This encourages me to pray for the well-being of my nation, recognizing that its prosperity affects all its inhabitants.

The story of Daniel provides a powerful example of interceding for leaders and nations. Daniel prayed earnestly for his people and their leaders, seeking God's intervention and wisdom. In Daniel 9:3, it is written, *"So I turned to the Lord God and pleaded with him in prayer and petition, in fasting, and in sackcloth and ashes."* Daniel's commitment to prayer and his intercession for his people highlight the importance of seeking God's help for national and global matters.

Another example is the prayer of Nehemiah for Jerusalem. Nehemiah's heartfelt prayer for his city and its leaders demonstrates the significance of praying for the restoration and guidance of nations. Nehemiah 1:5–6 records his plea:

> Then I said: "Lord, the God of heaven, the great and awesome God, who keeps his covenant of love with those who love him and keep his commandments, let your ear be attentive and your eyes open to hear the prayer your servant is praying before you day and night for your servants, the people of Israel."

Nehemiah's prayer underscores the importance of seeking God's favour and guidance for our communities and leaders.

Ultimately, I pray for God's will to be done in all aspects of governance and global affairs. Matthew 6:10 teaches us to pray in this manner: *"Your kingdom come, your will be done, on earth as it is in heaven."* I seek to align my prayers with God's purposes and trust that His plan for the world will unfold according to His divine will.

I also reflect on my own role in contributing to positive change and support for my country and the world. Micah 6:8 instructs, *"He has shown you, O mortal, what is good. And what does the Lord require of you? To act justly and to love mercy and to walk humbly with your God."* I ask God to help me fulfill my responsibilities and make a difference in my community.

In Romans 13: 1–7, the Word of God instructed me in this:

> Let everyone be subject to the governing authorities, for there is no authority except that which God has established. The authorities that exist have been established by God. Consequently, whoever rebels against the authority is rebelling against what God has instituted, and those who do so will bring judgment

on themselves. For rulers hold no terror for those who do right, but for those who do wrong. Do you want to be free from fear of the one in authority? Then do what is right and you will be commended. For the one in authority is God's servant for your good. But if you do wrong, be afraid, for rulers do not bear the sword for no reason. They are God's servants, agents of wrath to bring punishment on the wrongdoer. Therefore, it is necessary to submit to the authorities, not only because of possible punishment but also as a matter of conscience.

This is also why you pay taxes, for the authorities are God's servants, who give their full time to governing. Give to everyone what you owe them: If you owe taxes, pay taxes; if revenue, then revenue; if respect, then respect; if honor, then honor.

Therefore, I ought to lift them in prayer. By dedicating special prayers for governments, leaders, and global issues, I seek to support and uplift the world in which we live, asking for God's guidance and intervention in shaping a better future for all.

Part Four
THE TWELVE STEPS WITH JESUS

I have used the twelve-step recovery process as a reference throughout this book. For those unaware of these steps, I would like to provide a snapshot.

I have been grateful to be a member of the 12 Steps with Jesus fellowship group, which has provided me a unique way of incorporating prayer into my journey. Here is how each step aligns with the Christian faith:

1. Admitting powerlessness. In step one, I admit that I am powerless over sin and that my life has become unmanageable. Accepting Christ as our Lord and Savior is a one-time event, but every day is an opportunity to recognize our dependency on God's grace.

This step calls us to humility, reminding us of James 1:17: *"Every good and perfect gift is from above, coming down from the Father of the heavenly lights, who does not change like shifting shadows."* This verse helps me embrace a posture of surrender rather than boasting, acknowledging that without God there is nothing I can do.

The story of the apostle Paul in 2 Corinthians 12:9 illustrates this principle. Paul acknowledged his weakness and relied on God's strength, saying, *"But he said to me, 'My grace is sufficient for you, for my power is made perfect in weakness.'"*

2. Believing in a higher power. In step two, I come to believe that a power greater than myself, whom I call my perfect heavenly Father, can restore me to sanity. This helps me place God at the centre of my life, understanding that true fulfillment comes from Him alone. It reminds me that no person, place, or thing can replace the role of God in my life.

This is why I have chosen to confess my sin and believe, as stated in Romans 10:9, *"If you declare with your mouth, 'Jesus is Lord,' and believe in your heart that God raised him from the dead, you will be saved."*

The story of King Solomon's request for wisdom in reflects this step. Solomon recognized his need for divine guidance and sought God's wisdom above all else: *"So give your servant a discerning heart to govern your people and to distinguish between right and wrong"* (1 Kings 3:9).

3. Turning over our will. In step three, I make the decision to turn my will and life over to the care of God, as revealed through the sacrifice of Jesus Christ. While accepting Christ initially is a one-time event, each day we can recommit our lives to Him, seeking His guidance.

The dedication of Jesus to God's will in the garden of Gethsemane in Matthew 26:39 demonstrates this step. Jesus prayed, *"My Father, if it is possible, may this cup be taken from me. Yet not as I will, but as you will."* Jesus freely consented to come to the earth as a human to give us eternal life. In a similar way, we continually turn over our will to God to be our everything.

4. Conducting a moral inventory. In step four, I take a searching and fearless moral inventory of myself. By examining both my strengths and shortcomings, I prepare to work on improving myself with God's help. This step is about acknowledging my faults and seeking God's assistance in making necessary changes.

I pray Psalm 139:23–24 over my life. I ask of God, *"Search me, God, and know my heart; test me and know my anxious thoughts. See if there is any offensive way in me, and lead me in the way everlasting."*

King David's self-examination and repentance also exemplify this step. He prayed, *"Create in me a pure heart, O God, and renew a steadfast spirit within me"* (Psalm 51:10).

This step is crucial as it prompts me to look at the plank in my own eye instead of the speck of sawdust in my brothers' eye, as Matthew 7:3–5 instructs:

> Why do you look at the speck of sawdust in your brother's eye and pay no attention to the plank in your own eye? How can you say to your brother, "Let me take the speck out of your eye," when all the time there is a plank in your own eye? You hypocrite, first take the plank out of your own eye, and then you will see clearly to remove the speck from your brother's eye.

I am guilty of that. My own insecurity prompts me to try to change my spouse by fighting with him to remove the plank in his eye until the Lord brings me to a place of realizing that I am sometimes blind to the greater plank in my own. So it is important to conduct this inventory every day.

5. Confessing our wrongs. In step five, I admit to God, myself, and another person the exact nature of my wrongdoings, confessing my sins and seeking repentance. As James 5:16 instructs us, *"Therefore confess your sins to each other and pray for each other so that you may be healed."* This step helps me confront my faults without self-justification or blame.

The story of the prodigal son in Luke 15:21 shows the power of confession and repentance. In this story, the son says to his father, *"Father, I have sinned against heaven and against you. I am no longer worthy to be called your son."*

This is also a powerful encouragement for me, reminding me that however bad I fall, I can still go back to God and repent.

6. Being ready for God to remove our defects. In step six, I become entirely ready for God to remove all my defects of character. This step involves being willing to allow Him to transform me by addressing my flaws and imperfections. It requires me to be open to God's work in my life and desire to change.

The transformation of the apostle Peter in John 21:15–17 illustrates this readiness. Jesus asks Peter three times if he loves Him, each time commanding him the same way: *"Feed my lambs."* This demonstrates Peter's preparation to be restored and used by God despite his previous denials.

It is a fact that we cannot by our own power remove our defects. However, we can ask God for help and be confident that He will help us, while playing our part to make the work happen.

7. Humbly asking God to remove our shortcomings. In step seven, I humbly ask God to remove my shortcomings. This is an act of surrender and trust, acknowledging that I cannot overcome my flaws on my own but need divine intervention to make lasting changes.

In Philippians 4:13, Paul expresses this dependence on God: *"I can do all this through him who gives me strength."* This shows that even in our efforts to overcome shortcomings, we rely on God's power.

8. Making a list of those we have harmed. In step eight, I make a list of all the people I have harmed and become willing to make amends to them. This step emphasizes the importance of reconciliation and the healing that comes from acknowledging and addressing past wrongs.

The story of Zacchaeus in Luke 19:8–10 illustrates this step. Zacchaeus, a tax collector, acknowledges his past wrongs and commits to restoring what he has taken unjustly, demonstrating a willingness to make amends.

9. Making amends. In step nine, I make direct amends to such people wherever possible, except when to do so would injure them or others. This step focuses on actively seeking forgiveness and repairing relationships, recognizing the impact of our actions on others.

The story of Joseph and his brothers in Genesis 45:4–15 demonstrates the power of making amends. Joseph forgives his brothers for selling him into slavery and seeks reconciliation, demonstrating the healing that comes from making amends.

Just as I confess my sin to God, I am encouraged in these steps to confess my wrongs to the other people in my life, as long as it won't create more hurt. I must also repent, which means promising not to commit the same offence again. This is a powerful step for healing and moving forward.

10. Continuing to take a personal inventory. In step ten, I continue to take a personal inventory and promptly admit when I am wrong. This step emphasizes ongoing self-reflection and accountability, ensuring that I remain aware of my actions and their impact.

The apostle Paul's self-reflection in 1 Corinthians 9:27 exemplifies this step: *"No, I strike a blow to my body and make it my slave so that after I have preached to others, I myself will not be disqualified for the prize."* Paul's commitment to continual self-examination and discipline reflects this principle.

11. Seeking through prayer and meditation. In step eleven, I seek through prayer and meditation to improve my conscious contact with God, praying only for knowledge of His will and the power to carry it out. This step focuses on deepening our relationship with God through prayer, meditation, and seeking His guidance in our daily lives.

Jesus's practice of prayer and meditation can be seen in Luke 5:16: *"But Jesus often withdrew to lonely places and prayed."* This demonstrates the importance of seeking God's guidance and maintaining a close relationship with Him.

12. Carrying the message and practicing these principles. In step twelve, we carry the message to others and practice these principles in all our affairs. This step involves sharing the transformative power of our experiences and continuing to apply the principles of the program in every aspect of our lives.

The great commission illustrates this step. Jesus instructs His disciples to *"go and make disciples of all nations"* (Matthew 28:19), demonstrating the importance of sharing the message of faith and living out its principles.

Conclusion
A LIFE LED BY PRAYER

As we reach the conclusion of this journey of exploring the power of prayer, I want to leave you with a heartfelt reminder of the profound essence of this sacred practice. Prayer isn't merely a ritual or formality; it's an outflow of our profound and personal relationship with the Creator. Through prayer, we build and nurture this relationship, drawing closer to God and aligning our lives with His divine will. Prayer changes everything, starting with ourselves. It transforms our hearts, minds, and circumstances, connecting us with the Creator of the universe and providing us with the strength to face each day with hope and purpose.

Each section of this book has explored different facets of prayer, demonstrating how prayer intersects with every aspect of our lives. From the intimate moments of breath prayers to expansive global intercessions, we have seen prayer as an invitation to engage deeply with God, seek His guidance, and express our heartfelt desires and concerns.

James 1:27 reminds us of the true essence of the religion that God values: *"Religion that God our Father accepts as pure and faultless is this: to look after orphans and widows in their distress and to keep oneself from being polluted by the world."* This verse calls us to a genuine and compassionate faith expressed through our actions and prayers. It's not about following rituals for the sake of tradition but about living out our faith in meaningful ways.

Prayer is about relationship. It's about seeking God's presence, aligning our hearts with His, and trusting Him with every part of our lives. It's an act of love, commitment, and surrender. As we pray for ourselves, our loved ones, and our world, we engage in a divine dialogue that shapes us and the world around us.

As you move forward, remember that prayer is a continuous journey, not a destination. It is a daily practice of drawing near to God, seeking His guidance, and finding comfort in His presence. Whether you're praying for personal needs, interceding for others, or seeking wisdom for your plans, know that your prayers are heard and valued by God.

I pray that this book has served as a guide and encouragement in your journey to cultivate a vibrant prayer life. Let your prayers be filled with faith, hope, and love, knowing that through them you are connecting with the one who knows you intimately and desires to walk with you through every moment of your life.

In every prayer, remember that you are not alone. You are part of a larger community of believers, all seeking God's grace and guidance.

In closing, I want to remind you that God has made the following promise:

> Truly I tell you, whatever you bind on earth will be bound in heaven, and whatever you loose on earth will be loosed in heaven.
> Again, truly I tell you that if two of you on earth agree about anything they ask for, it will be done for them by my Father in heaven. For where two or three gather in my name, there am I with them.

Together, let us continue to uplift each other in prayer, strive to live out our faith with sincerity, and embrace the transformative power of a life led by prayer.

I pray that this book has been a source of encouragement for you. May these prayers become a part of your daily life, guiding you as you seek to live out your faith with intention and devotion.

Remember, no prayer is too small or insignificant in God's eyes. He delights in our prayers and is faithful to answer them in His perfect timing. As you continue your journey, may you always be guided by faith, trusting in God's unwavering love and grace.

> *Remember, no prayer is too small or insignificant in God's eyes. He delights in our prayers and is faithful to answer them in His perfect timing.*

ABOUT THE AUTHOR

Sephora Pierre-Louis is an adventurous woman who embraces risk-taking and exhibits a remarkable passion for exceeding expectations. With a proven ability to navigate complex interpersonal relationships, she exudes poise, confidence, and maturity in every interaction. She excels in establishing meaningful connections based on respect and trust, approaching each person she encounters with integrity, equity, inclusivity, and respect. To her, every relationship is an opportunity for learning and growth.

Sephora holds a bachelor's degree in computerized management from Ecole Supérieure d'Infotronique d'Haïti, a bachelor's degree in theology from Ministère Pêcheurs d'Homme, a master's degree in divinity from Liberty University, and a master's degree in project management from Université Quisqueya. She also has an associate's degree in psychology from the Université du Québec à Montréal and an MBA from Mills College in California. A distinguished Toastmaster and lifelong learner, Sephora continually hones her communication and leadership skills.

With a deep commitment to her professional journey, Sephora is a writer and trainer in management, communication, marketing, leadership, entrepreneurship, civic education, conflict resolution, personal development, and coaching. She is an active member of Ward Memorial Baptist Church, where she leads weekly Bible studies and guides the women's ministry.

Her key to success lies in recognizing our true self and aspiring identity. She sees herself foremost as a citizen of heaven, a daughter of the King of Kings, the almighty God of the universe. This identity shapes her life, inspiring her to reflect her heavenly Father's values. The Bible is her constant source of inspiration, guiding her to cultivate the fruits of the Spirit: love, joy, peace, patience, kindness, goodness, faithfulness, gentleness, and self-control. This spiritual foundation anchors her in a world often marked by discrimination and despair.

As a devoted mother, Sephora tirelessly advocates for her children, whom she cherishes as her most precious gifts. Her infectious smile and vibrant energy are matched by her unwavering humility, a value she holds dear. She attributes her successes to a life dedicated to God while attentively considering the guidance and needs of those around her.

Optimism radiates from her and she firmly believes that every individual contributes to the progress of others, even those who may judge or criticize. To her, failure is merely the act of not rising after a fall. In the face of setbacks, she describes herself as stubborn, as she perseveres, starts anew, and never surrenders. She embodies a spirit that transcends boundaries.

Sephora's dream is a world filled with peace, free from hatred, war, and suffering. Grounded in steadfast values rooted in love, she encourages others to leave the past behind, embrace the present, and focus on the future. Her greatest counsel to her contemporaries is to leave a legacy of a better life for future generations.

Website: https://www.sephorapierrelouis.com/
Facebook: https://www.facebook.com/bdeuxchange/
Instagram: @bdeuxchange
Twitter: @bdeuxchange